BACKROAD BICYCLING
in Eastern Pennsylvania

BACKROAD BICYCLING
in Eastern Pennsylvania

25 Rides for Touring and Mountain Bikes

Patricia Vance

Backcountry Guides
Woodstock · Vermont

With time, road numbers, signs, park regulations, and amenities may change. If you find that such changes have occurred along the routes described in this book, please let the author and publisher know so that corrections may be made in future editions. Other comments and suggestions are also welcome. Address all correspondence to:

Editor, Backroad Bicycle Tours
Backcountry Guides
P.O. Box 748
Woodstock, VT 05091

Library of Congress Cataloging-in-Publication Data

Vance, Patricia.
Backroad bicycling in eastern Pennsylvania : 25 rides for touring and mountain bikes / Patricia Vance. —1st ed.
          p. cm.
    ISBN 0-88150-477-7 (alk. paper)
    1. Bicycle touring—Pennsylvania—Guidebooks. 2. Pennsylvania—Guidebooks. I. Title.
GV1045.5.P4   V36 2001
917.48—dc21

00–069123

Cover design by Bodenweber Design
Text design by Sally Sherman
Cover and interior photographs by Patricia Vance
Maps by Inkspot: A Design Company, © 2001 The Countryman Press
Published by The Countryman Press, P.O. Box 748, Woodstock, Vermont 05091
Distributed by W. W. Norton & Company, Inc., 500 Fifth Avenue, New York, NY 10110
Printed in the United States of America

10 9 8 7 6 5 4 3 2 1

Dedication

This book is dedicated to my mother
who took off the training wheels and let go.

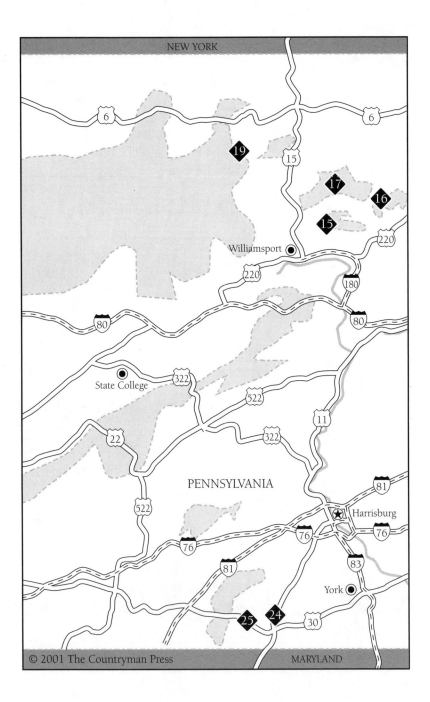

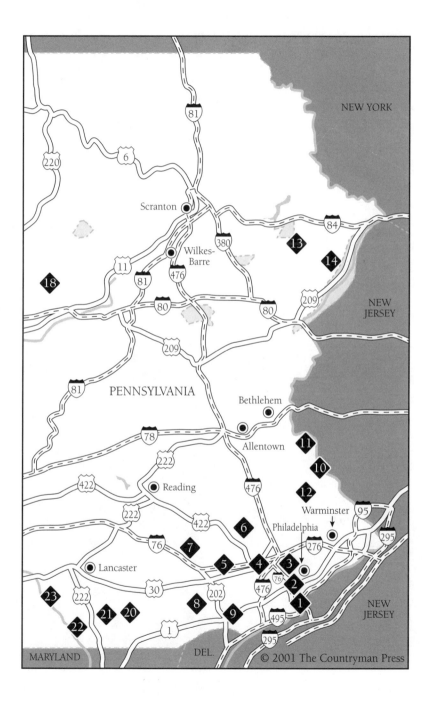

Contents

V. THE POCONOS

VI. THE ENDLESS MOUNTAINS

VII. PENNSYLVANIA DUTCH COUNTRY

VIII. HILLS ALONG THE SUSQUEHANNA RIVER

IX. GETTYSBURG, THE TURNING POINT OF THE CIVIL WAR

Acknowledgments

I want to thank the many members of the Bicycle Club of Philadelphia for information about their favorite roads and trails. Special thanks to Susan Cohen, Dave Johnson, and Mark Spangler.

For inspiration and encouragement, thanks to the Art Night Gang, the Ladies's Hiking and Outdoor Society, and Men's Auxiliary, my fellow lab rats, and my wonderful Woodlawn Street neighbors.

My thanks to Michael Parente, for introducing me to the joys of bicycling in Pennsylvania and for more than 20 years of contented eccentricity. We have fun.

Thanks to my sister, Beth, for decades of talk, from soul-baring confessions to idle chatter.

Backroad Bicycle Tours at a Glance

Tour	Region	Distance
1. Old City	Philadelphia	10
2. Fairmount Houses	Philadelphia	12
3. The Drives	Philadelphia	28
4. Freedom Valley Bike Trail	Valley Forge	19
5. Valley Forge National Park	Valley Forge	30
6. Evansburg State Park	Valley Forge	33
7. French Creek State Park	Valley Forge	49
8. Brandywine Creek	Brandywine River Valley	14
9. Ridley Creek State Park	Brandywine River Valley	37
10. Delaware Canal Towpath	Bucks County	30
11. Ringing Rocks	Bucks County	26
12. Arts and Crafts in Bucks County	Bucks County	40
13. Promised Land State Park	Poconos	55
14. Pocono Mountain Ramble	Poconos	32
15. Rolling Foothills	Endless Mountains	33
16. World's End State Park	Endless Mountains	39
17. Sullivan Mountain Sleigh Ride	Endless Mountains	23
18. Covered Bridge Tour	Endless Mountains	38
19. The Grand Canyon of Pennsylvania	Endless Mountains	36
20. Scenic Octoraro Creek	Pennsylvania Dutch	27
21. Amish Farmlands	Pennsylvania Dutch	28
22. Tuquan Creek	Susquehanna River	26
23. Conestoga Creek	Susquehanna River	23
24. East Cavalry Battlefield	Gettysburg	43
25. National Military Park Tour	Gettysburg	40

Difficulty	Bicycle	Highlights
Easy	Any	Independence National Park
Easy	Any	Historic houses
Easy	Mtn./hybrid	Fairmount Park
Easy	Any	Rail trail along Schuylkill River
Easy	Any	Valley Forge National Park
Moderate	Any	Evansburg State Park
Moderate/Difficult	Any	Hopewell Furnace National Historic Site
Easy	Any	Longwood Gardens
Moderate/Difficult	Any	Tyler Arboretum
Easy	Mtn./hybrid	Delaware River Canal Towpath
Easy/Moderate	Mtn./hybrid	Ringing rocks
Moderate	Any	Peace Valley Nature Center
Moderate	Any	Mountain bike trails
Moderate	Any	Scenery along Delaware River
Moderate/Difficult	Any	Wooded hills
Moderate	Mtn./hybrid	Loyalsock Canyon Vista & High Knob Overlook
Moderate	Mtn./hybrid	Wooded logging roads
Difficult	Mtn./hybrid	Ricketts Glen State Park
Difficult	Mtn./hybrid	Pine Creek
Moderate	Any	Octoraro Creek
Moderate/Difficult	Any	Beautiful Amish farms
Moderate/Difficult	Any	Shenk's Ferry Wildflower Preserve
Moderate	Any	Birdwatching in Safe Harbor marshes
Moderate	Any	National Cemetery and historic battle sites
Moderate/Difficult	Any	Gettysburg Battlefield Auto Tour

Introduction

I have a vivid memory of my first sight of Pennsylvania. After spending the first twenty-five years of my life in Minneapolis, Minnesota, I stuffed as much as I could into my eight-year-old Mercury Comet and headed east to graduate school in New Jersey. Not long after I crossed the Ohio/Pennsylvania border in the wee hours of the morning, I pulled into a rest stop to sleep for a bit, curled up in the front seat. At dawn, I poured down a large cup of coffee, washed my face, brushed my teeth, and pushed on. It was very foggy, and I felt the rise and fall of the Appalachian Mountains before I saw them. The mist separated and settled into the valleys, giving me glorious views from the summits. As I rolled up and down the heavily wooded hills, carpeted with dense, lush greenery, I fell in love.

I met my husband, Michael, at Rutgers University in New Jersey. He is a Philadelphia native, and we moved there after we graduated in 1982. Through the years I have read about Philadelphia and Pennsylvania in ways that natives never do. It is the outsider who comes to stay who really studies a place. Riding bicycles through and around Pennsylvania, Michael and I taught each other much and discovered more together. I hope these rides will give you a taste of my beautiful and fascinating adopted home.

The Land

Eastern Pennsylvania has a varied topography including the relatively flat coastal plain that extends from the Atlantic Ocean through Philadelphia and on to the Susquehanna River. Most of Pennsylvania's richest farmland lies in this area. This is also the birthplace of modern Pennsylvania, and you can trace the history of European colonization through the streets of Philadelphia and other southeastern towns. This region is by no means completely flat, but this is where you will find the easiest rides in this book.

To the west of the Susquehanna River the foothills of the Appalachian Mountains begin. Harrisburg, the state's capital, is conveniently situ-

Hopewell Furnace National Historic Site contains buildings from a 19th-century village, a restored cold-blast furnace and a working water wheel.

ated in a gap, making it accessible from both the east and the west. Gettysburg, in the south, is located on a tiny finger of the Blue Ridge Mountains. These ridges played an important role in the outcome of the Battle of Gettysburg, as you will see in the last two chapters. The land around Gettysburg is also fertile, and some of Pennsylvania's best orchards roll up and down the hills here.

Moving north and west, the hills continue to rise and fall into long parallel ridges. The ripples become higher and steeper through the Pocono and the Endless Mountains. This land was logged, frequently clear-cut, for over a century. The soil resisted cultivation, causing many early settlements to fail. However, it is to our advantage in the long run, as these wooded hills are beautiful places to visit, especially by bicycle.

The Climate

The four seasons are markedly different in Pennsylvania. Average summer temperatures in the south are in the mid-80s. In the north, both latitude and altitude decrease that by about 5 degrees. It is not unusual to experience temperatures above 90 in July and August with accompanying humidity.

In January, average temperatures are in the mid-30s in the south, while they can be in the mid-20s farther north.

There are about 10 days with precipitation amounting to 3 to 4 inches per month throughout the year and throughout the eastern half of the state.

Spring and autumn are frequently perfect for a bicycling excursion. Mild temperatures, many days of sunshine, and beautiful scenery make these my favorite times of the year for vacations.

Autumn in Pennsylvania is a delight. It is not just the intensity of the colors but the variety that dazzles. Fall color is stunning from Philadelphia to Gettysburg to Scranton to Williamsport. Pennsylvania is one of the most heavily wooded states in the country, although there are only a few small areas of virgin timber. The north and south hardwood regions meet here, yielding a great variety of trees.

Mountain laurel is the state flower, and it is at its best in late May and early to mid-June. Its cousins, azaleas and rhododendrons, are also spectacular in the spring.

The People

The first inhabitants of what is now Pennsylvania arrived 6,000 to 8,000 years ago. The earliest evidence of human habitation is pictographs on islands in the Susquehanna River. Little else is known about the people who carved them.

When Europeans arrived in the 17th century, the Susquehanna Indians, for whom the river was named, occupied this area. A second group of Indians lived along the Atlantic coast from Cape Henlopen, Delaware, to Long Island, New York. However, the largest population lived along the Delaware River. Since Europeans had already named the river, they decided to call the people the Delaware Indians. The Indians called

A scenic country road in Evansburg.

themselves the Leni-Lenape (LEN-ee len-AH-pay), or "original people."

William Penn is considered by many to be one of the few Europeans who dealt with the Indians with respect and honesty. Penn was the son of a British admiral. King Charles II of England owed a debt to the senior Penn and in 1681 paid it off by deeding land in the American colonies to the son. Charles sought to accomplish two goals with this action: he paid off a debt and he sent a troublesome group of religious activists off to the wilderness.

Penn was a Quaker, a group that was persecuted in Europe, and he enacted laws guaranteeing tolerance for all religions in Pennsylvania. In accordance with Quaker beliefs, Penn attempted to deal with the Leni-Lenape fairly.

Penn's sons and their representatives did not hold the same values, however. After Penn left the colonies for the last time in 1701, the Leni-Lenape suffered the same persecution and forced migration that befell so many North American Indians. Today there are about 2,000 Leni-Lenape living in Oklahoma. A smaller group resides in Ontario.

The Susquehanna Indians fared much worse than the Leni-Lenape. They were killed in large numbers in war with the Iroquois in the late 17th century. Then in December 1763, a gang of drunken rangers from

Paxton, Pennsylvania slaughtered the last 20 members, exterminating the entire culture.

European culture quickly dominated in Pennsylvania. Philadelphia became one of the largest cities in the colonies. The Delaware Bay became, and still remains, one of the most active shipping areas in the world. Farms produced goods that were distributed throughout the colonies and Europe. The Continental Congress met in Philadelphia in 1771, and Philadelphia was the young nation's capital from 1790 to 1800. The hills are rich with iron; mining and manufacturing became booming industries in the 19th century. Manufacturing enriched Philadelphians while the arts and culture flourished.

All during its history, immigrants have come to Penn's "holy experiment" for economic opportunity and religious freedom. This is still occurring today, although the city has also suffered from suburban flight and neglect, like so many other U.S. cities.

Chapters

I have tried to include some flat, easy rides in this book, but there are only a few places in eastern Pennsylvania where this can be accomplished. Even though Philadelphia lies on the coastal plain, the Schuylkill and Delaware Rivers etched gorges in the land where it yields to the Appalachian Mountains. You have to ride up and down quite a few hills to see the lovely scenery along the rivers. This is true even along the broad, shallow Susquehanna River. The farther west and north you go, the higher the hills and the deeper the valleys.

But don't despair. The rides take a bit more muscle, but they're worth it. The most beautiful scenery is almost always hilly, and this is certainly true of Pennsylvania.

I have organized each chapter in the same way. You will find a brief introduction to the area, followed by a mile-by-mile description of the route.

Difficulty

Each ride is graded as easy, moderate, or difficult. In an easy route, there are few or no hills, and the distance is short enough to be completed in a couple of hours by even a slow cyclist. However, that doesn't mean it won't take several hours to enjoy the scenery or visit attractions along the way.

A moderate ride will be longer and have some hills and climbs.

A difficult ride is long, has many hills, several climbs, or a combination of all of these.

Terrain

This includes a description of the topography. A hill is a rise of over 200 feet over any distance. A climb is a rise of over 500 feet and/or a hill that continues for over 1 mile. That is, a climb is a particularly long and/or steep hill.

"Rolling" does not mean "small hills." It means that you will be going up and down frequently. If the hills are small I use the term "gently rolling." Sometimes the hills are significant, and they just keep coming at you. I have called this "rolling throughout." "Moderately rolling" means you will face several significant hills, but not all the time. If I call a ride "hilly throughout," I do not describe each hill. Expect to be pushing up and then coasting down for the entire ride.

It is difficult to rate a ride with a system that is agreed upon by everyone who rides it. I have tried to be objective and to define my terms as clearly as I can. Ultimately, however, what is hard for me may be very different from what is hard for you. I suggest if you are fairly new to biking that you begin with one of the easier rides so you can see how you would rate that ride before you try any of the difficult ones.

I find it helpful to know when the hard parts are coming and when they are over, so I have included the location of significant hills and noted where the summit of each is.

This section also includes a description of the type of roads and road surfaces you can expect to encounter. If there are any unpaved roads or sections, I let you know.

I have also indicated which rides would be better suited to a mountain bike or a hybrid. This distinction is due mostly to the quality of the road surface. None of these rides are on trails or singletrack.

Of Special Interest

In this section, I describe attractions or points of interest that are located on or near the route that you may find interesting. I have included hours of operation when appropriate, along with addresses and phone numbers.

Location

This is the town or site where the ride begins and ends. All routes are circles, bringing you back to your starting point. I have included an approximate distance to the four largest population centers in eastern Pennsylvania: Philadelphia, Allentown, Harrisburg, and Scranton. These are approximations to help you judge the time it will take to get to the starting point from about the middle of the city in question.

To Get There

This includes directions from one or two of the closest interstate highways to the starting point. Directions will take you to a place to park your car while you ride.

Services

Places along the route where you can get food and drinks are listed here. You will also find some suggestions for overnight lodging, including hotels, B&Bs, camping, and hostels. There is also information about food stores and restaurants near the route. The location of a nearby bike shop is listed.

The Ride

The distance to each change of direction is listed, followed by instructions and descriptions. In the additional comments, I give landmarks or other information to help you navigate your way through the area. Sometimes I include additional information about the area.

Each time you need to change direction, there is a mileage listing and a description. Read all the information so you won't miss navigational details, interesting facts and factoids, or my droll wit.

Optional routes

In many chapters, I have included some options to make routes longer or shorter. You can also link routes to put together a weekend or more. I have included a few suggestions about joining routes and places to stay overnight.

Maintenance and Repair

It is worthwhile and not difficult to become familiar with the general mechanisms of a bicycle. Bikes are held together with a bunch of screws, bolts, and nuts, and once you get the general idea it's pretty easy to figure out how to deal with basic road repairs. There are many good books available. I especially like Tom Cuthbertson's *Anybody's Bike Book and Bike Bag Book*. There are also many bike shops that offer workshops on bike repair; many do not charge a fee.

Whether you want to become a good bike mechanic or not, it is absolutely necessary to be able to cope with a flat tire if you ride a bike. You should always carry a pump and a patch kit. In addition, I strongly recommend a spare tube and a tire lever. You can buy all of these inexpensively and stuff them into a saddlebag behind your seat. If you prefer a larger pump, there are many that will attach directly to the bike frame so you don't need a large pack. I prefer patches that need glue because they are stronger, but the glueless ones are fine for small holes in tires that are not extremely high pressure, that is, less than 100 pounds per square inch (psi).

Fixing a flat tire is easy. You can even patch a tire without removing the wheel. Here are the steps:
- Pry the tire off the rim with the tire lever.
- Pull out the tube.
- Pump it up to find the hole.
- Let the air out.
- Rough up the spot with the sandpaper that comes in the patch kit.
- Apply the glue to an area larger than the size of the patch.

- Wait five minutes.
- Put the patch over the glue using your fingernails to rub the patch down well.
- Pump up the tube to make sure the patch is holding.
- Let most, but not all of the air out. This makes it easier to put back into the tire.
- When the tube is back in place, use your tire lever to re-seat the tire.

I carry a bicycle multi-tool designed to be small enough to fit into a saddlebag; it includes many of the tools you will most likely need for road repairs. Mine has a set of Allen wrenches, a couple of common box wrenches, a chain tool, spoke wrench, Philips and straight screwdriver, and a small knife blade.

Safety

Wear a helmet. All helmets that are approved by ASNI and the Snell Foundation are safe. The higher-priced models have more style, better fit, less weight, more ventilation, an aerodynamic shape or a famous name, but they are not safer. Check your helmet regularly for cracks and dents and replace it if you see any. But helmets can be structurally damaged even if they look perfect, so replace yours if you take a fall and hit your head. Sunlight and day-to-day wear and tear will also weaken a helmet, so replace yours every five years regardless of its history. Never buy or sell a used helmet.

I
PHILADELPHIA: CITY TOURS

Philadelphia: City Tours

The city of Philadelphia started as William Penn's "holy experiment" to create a place where all religions could be practiced freely. In 1681, King Charles II of England gave Penn land in the colonies to repay a debt owed to Penn's father. It was a politically motivated payment designed to get the pesky, radical Quaker out of England.

The first site Penn chose for his town was south of Philadelphia, on the Delaware River near the mouth of the Schuylkill River, close to the current location of the Philadelphia International Airport. However, Penn's scout and surveyor found that Swedish immigrants had already established homes and farms there. While disputes over land deeded in Europe caused many problems in the New World, the peace-loving Quakers decided not to push the issue and sailed north up the Delaware River a few miles. They established Philadelphia in the area with the shortest distance between the two rivers.

As early as 1600, Europeans arriving in this area encountered people who called themselves the Leni-Lenape (LEN-ee len-AH-pay), or "original people." Penn and his first advisors worked with the Leni-Lenape to reach an agreement that was satisfactory to both sides. By paying with goods, Penn purchased a tract of land for new immigrants.

Unfortunately for the Lenape, Penn returned to England for good in 1701. In 1737, his sons and their representatives decided the original agreement was inadequate and conned the Lenape into giving them more land. The Penns drew up a phony document and told the Lenape that their ancestors had signed an agreement with Penn's ancestors and had agreed to give up as much land as could be walked in a day and a half. The Lenape, as honorable, peace-loving people, respected the sham treaty. Rather than allow the Lenape to accompany them on a casual walk from Philadelphia along the river on established trails, the Europeans employed professional messengers to run the shortest distance, stopping only for brief rests. Only one man lasted for the day and a half, but he covered over 58 miles. The Lenape knew they had been cheated, but integrity and honesty compelled them to uphold the Walking Purchase.

The Leni-Lenape continued to be pushed east throughout the next 130 years until most ended up on reservations in Oklahoma. While many Indians were relocated to Oklahoma, most were able to keep their population together to retain autonomy as a nation. Since there were so few Lenape, they were placed on the same reservation as the Cherokee, making it more difficult to preserve their culture. A small group fled to Canada in 1890, and their ancestors live on two small reserves in Ontario.

In the 17th century, the earliest Europeans lived in caves along the Delaware River until houses were built, the first of which were simple log cabins. Many of the English immigrants had witnessed the Great Fire of London in 1666; fireproof building materials were used extensively to avoid any similar disaster here. The soil in this part of Pennsylvania has very high red clay content, and red brick became Philadelphia's most popular building material.

William Penn designed a grid of lots that spanned the two rivers, but the woods were dense and it was easier to expand north and south along the Delaware River. Most of the area's oldest buildings are within a few blocks of the river, and you will see them on the Old City tour (chapter 1). The city did not reach west to the Schuylkill River until around 1825. However, by the mid-1700s, there were scattered country estates along the high bluffs of the Schuylkill, and you will visit some of these on the "Fairmount Park Houses" tour (chapter 2).

Outlying communities existed before 1800, notably Germantown, Frankford, and Manayunk. As you cycle "The Drives" in chapter 3, you will see the beautiful Wissahickon Valley in the Germantown section of the city. You will also pass through Manayunk, a former 19th-century industrial shantytown that is now a mecca of excellent restaurants and boutiques.

Location: The ride begins and ends at the Philadelphia Museum of Art at Eakins Oval and the Ben Franklin Parkway in Philadelphia. It is located 62 miles south of Allentown, 105 miles east of Harrisburg, 125 miles south of Scranton.

Of Special Interest: The Philadelphia Museum of Art (215-684-7500) is open Tuesday through Sunday from 10 AM to 5 PM. Admission is charged except on Sunday before 1 PM.

The Azalea Garden on Aquarium Drive is at its peak in late spring. This is a popular place for wedding photos, and you may find more than one party roaming among the blossoms in formal gowns and tuxes.

Services: Lloyd Hall, next to the parking lot on Aquarium Drive, sells snacks and beverages and has public toilets. Philadelphia has the complete range of hotels, guest houses, and B&Bs you would expect from a large city. The phone number for the Tourist Promotion Agency in Philadelphia is 1-800-537-7676. They can help you with reservations. For something a bit unusual, try the charming and elegant Society Hill Hotel B&B at 301 Chestnut Street; 215-925-1919.

The Bank Street Hostel makes a pleasant, inexpensive, and very convenient place to stay in the center of town. The address is 32 South Bank Street; 215-922-0222. In Fairmount Park on Chamounix Drive, try the Chamounix Mansion Hostel; 215-878-3676.

1
Old City

Distance: 10 miles

Difficulty: Easy

Terrain: Flat and paved throughout. You will encounter traffic on some sections of the ride. Be sure you are familiar with traffic laws and are comfortable sharing the road with cars. Suitable for any bicycle.

Location: The ride begins and ends at the Philadelphia Museum of Art at Eakins Oval and the Ben Franklin Parkway in Philadelphia. It is located 62 miles south of Allentown, 105 miles east of Harrisburg, 125 miles south of Scranton.

Of Special Interest: The Rodin Museum, at 21st Street and Ben Franklin Parkway, is open Tuesday through Sunday from 10–5. Admission is charged.

The Franklin Institute and Science Museum at Race and 21st Streets is open at least 9:30–5 daily. The science museum has regular planetarium shows and an IMAX theater. Admission is charged.

Most of the buildings in Independence National Park are open daily 9–5, as is Christ Church on 2nd and Market Streets. Franklin Court museums, 3rd and Market Streets, are open 10–4.

Services: There are many places to stop for food. Lloyd Hall, next to the parking lot on Aquarium Drive, sells snacks and beverages and has public toilets. Some of the best pizza in town is served at Mama Palma's Restaurant at 23rd and Spruce Streets. My favorite Philadelphia deli, Food-Tek, is on 2nd Street between Market and Chestnut Streets. For excellent ice cream, stop at Bonnie's at Front and Chestnut Streets.

Bicycle Shop: Bicycle Therapy is an excellent bike shop just a few blocks from 22nd and Spruce Street at 2211 South Street, 215-735-7849. They are open 10–6, 10–7 on Wednesday, closed Sunday.

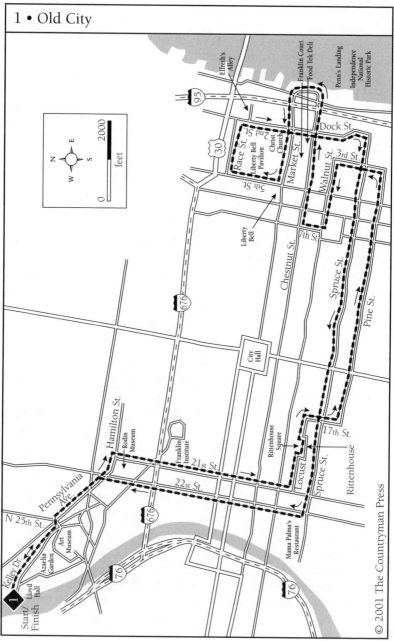

N
W — E
S

0 — 2000 feet

Elfreth's Alley
Franklin Court
Food Tek Deli
Penn's Landing
Independence National Historic Park

95

Dock St.

2nd St.
Christ Church
Race St.
Liberty Bell Pavilion

30

Market St.
Walnut St.
3rd St.

5th St.

Liberty Bell

Chestnut St.

7th St.

Spruce St.

Pine St.

676

City Hall

Hamilton St.
Rodin Museum

Franklin Institute

21st St.

Rittenhouse Square

17th St.

Spruce St.

Locust

Rittenhouse

22st St.

Pennsylvania Ave.

N 25th St.

676

Mama Palma's Restaurant

Keller Dr.

Art Museum

Azalea Garden

76

76

1

Start/ Finish

Lloyd Hall

© 2001 The Countryman Press

To Get There

From I-76 or I-90, take I-676 exit. Take I-676 to the Ben Franklin Parkway exit. Follow signs to the Parkway and the art museum. Bear right at Eakins Oval and go straight on Kelly Drive, keeping the art museum on your left. A small traffic circle goes around a two-story statue of Abraham Lincoln in the middle of Kelly Drive. Go left, following the circle behind Lincoln. Continue on Aquarium Drive, straight ahead. The parking lot is in 0.1 mile on the right.

You won't begin this ride in Old City, Philadelphia's colonial section. Instead, you will begin in the Fairmount neighborhood on the Schuylkill River, built in the 20th century. The Philadelphia Museum of Art, completed in 1928, is the dominant structure in the area. It was the last phase of construction of Ben Franklin Parkway.

Then you will ride east to the Delaware River, traveling back in time as you go. The buildings around the art museum are 20th-century structures. They will get older as you ride east. The next highlight is the neighborhood around Rittenhouse Square, built by wealthy Philadelphians in the 19th century. A few blocks before the Delaware River, you will arrive in the 18th century and visit Independence National Park, including the old State House where the Declaration of Independence was signed.

None of the original log cabins built by the first European settlers remain on the riverbanks. Instead, you'll see Penn's Landing, a thoroughly modern seaport with many interesting sights.

The Ride

0.0 Left from the parking lot on Aquarium Drive.

0.1 Right on the bike path on Kelly Drive.

0.3 Left at the second traffic light on 25th Street. Immediately turn right and go through the parking area.

This is Pennsylvania Avenue. At 22nd Street and Pennsylvania Avenue, look to your left at the Parkway House, a wonderful example of Art Deco and International style architecture constructed in 1952.

0.7 Follow the main road to the left where Pennsylvania Avenue becomes Hamilton Street.

0.7 Next right on 21st Street. The Rodin Museum is on the right.

1.0 At the traffic light, go straight across Ben Franklin Parkway.

By 1907, poverty and negligence had filled this section of the city with slums and derelict commercial buildings. In 1911, national experts in art, architecture, and city planning developed a bold, ambitious plan to construct what was called the "American Champs-Elysées." By 1917, the city had razed a 1-mile strip of land from City Hall to the river, and the project was finished in 1928 when the art museum opened.

The Franklin Institute and Science Museum is on the left between the Parkway and Race Street.

1.7 Left on Locust Street.

In 1875, noted architect Frank Furness designed the house on the north east corner. Furness pioneered the intricate red brickwork, ornate moldings and projections, and sculpted terra-cotta that characterized the Victorian era.

1.8 Right at the T on West Rittenhouse Square.

The buildings in this area were constructed during the 19th century when many of the city's wealthiest residents lived here.

1.9 Follow the road to the left on South Rittenhouse Square.

2.0 Continue with the road to the left on East Rittenhouse Square.

2.0 Immediately turn right on Locust Street.

The 1600 block is known for its elegant townhouses. Note the wonderful first-floor window frame on the brownstone at Number 1618.

2.3 Right on 17th Street.

2.5 Left on Pine Street.

3.5 Left on 3rd Street.

On Delancey Street, the Hill-Physick-Keith House, built in 1786, is an excellent example of Federal architecture. The house is open to the public 10–4 on Tuesday through Saturday, and on Sunday from 1–4.

Pennsylvania Hospital, the first hospital in the colonies, was founded in 1755. That's Philadelphia's favorite son, Benjamin Franklin, immortalized in the sculpture.

The Powell House, a wonderful Georgian row house built in 1765, is on Spruce Street, immediately after the Hill-Physick-Keith House, and is open at the same times.

3.8 Left on Walnut Street.

The Curtis Building is on the right at 4.0 miles. It houses the glass mosaic, *The Dream Garden,* constructed in 1916 by Louis Comfort Tiffany from a Maxfield Parrish oil painting. The Curtis Building is open during normal business hours, and *The Dream Garden* is worth a stop.

4.1 Right on 7th Street after passing Washington Square.

4.2 Right on Chestnut Street.

4.3 Independence Hall is between 5th and 6th Streets.

Originally the Pennsylvania State House, the Second Continental

Congress met here and the Declaration of Independence was signed in the Assembly Room. From 1790 to 1800 this was the capital building of the new government.

This national park is beautifully landscaped and there are charming buildings on the grounds. This is a good spot to walk your bike or lock it to a sturdy signpost and look around a bit before continuing. The visitor's center is on 3rd Street, between Chestnut and Walnut Streets.

If you are in the mood for a frozen treat, Bonnie's Ice Cream is at the corner of 2nd and Chestnut Streets.

4.8 Follow the elevated roadway to the left unless you want to stop at Penn's Landing.

There is a museum, the Port of History, and several historic ships that are open to the public.

4.9 Continue to follow the roadway to the left again, down to Market Street.

Franklin Court, a history of and tribute to Philadelphia's first citizen, is on the left at 5.2 miles.

There are many restored buildings and a museum with several exhibits in the area. Even if you do not stop, take a quick look at *Ghost Structures.* This sculpture is the full-sized, painted steel outline or "ghost" of Franklin's home and print shop, erected on the original site.

5.4 Right on 5th Street.

The Liberty Bell is on the opposite side of the park on 6th Street. The Atwater-Kent Museum is at 155 7th Street. This excellent museum specializes in Philadelphia history.

Just before you reach Race Street, look across the street to your left at the Noguchi sculpture, *Bolt of Lightning: A Memorial to Benjamin Franklin.*

5.6 Right on Race Street.

As you approach 2nd Street you will be treated to a great view of the Ben Franklin Bridge. By now you probably sense the love affair Philadelphia has with Franklin.

Even during his lifetime, he was the darling of the city and his image was everywhere. He wrote to a friend in 1780 that he had "sat so much and so often to Painters and Statuaries that I am perfectly sick of it." The first public work of art in Philadelphia, Francesco Lazzarini's statue of Franklin, was installed in 1792 in the facade of the Library Company at 1314 Locust Street. It was subsequently moved inside the building to protect it from exposure. From the University of Pennsylvania, which Franklin founded, to the Franklin Mint, to the *Bolt of Lightning*, Philadelphia pays fond tribute to its favorite son.

5.9 Right on 2nd Street.

6.0 Left on Elfreth's Alley, the oldest continuously occupied street in North America.

There is a small museum at #126, open from 10–4 daily. All of the other buildings are privately owned homes.

At the end of the alley, turn around and go back to 2nd Street.

6.1 Left on 2nd Street.

Christ Church is on the right at 6.3 miles. When it was constructed in 1744, it was considered to be the most beautiful building in the colonies.

If you are ready for lunch, try Food-Tek, a deli on the right after Market Street at 6.2 miles. Don't forget to lock your bike to a sturdy, permanent structure like a signpost.

6.6 Left where 2nd Street ends and Dock Street starts. Continue on Dock Street.

6.7 Right at the T on Spruce Street.

Pennsylvania Hospital is on 8th Street at 7.3 miles. Built in 1755, it is the oldest hospital in North America. Ben you-know-who helped with funding and planning.

On 9th and Spruce Streets you will find Portico Row, townhouses built in 1831 for upper-class professionals.

8.6 Right on 22nd Street.

If this is a better time for lunch, continue straight on Spruce for 1 block to Mama Palma's Restaurant on 23rd and Spruce Streets on the right.

9.6 Left on Pennsylvania Avenue after crossing Ben Franklin Parkway.

9.9 *Turn left at the traffic light onto 25th Street.*

Before you turn, take a look at the Fidelity Mutual Life Insurance Building straight ahead, one of the most beautiful Art Deco buildings in the city. The Philadelphia Museum of Art purchased it recently and intends to renovate it for museum exhibits. Cross Kelly Drive and turn right on the bike path.

10.2 *Left on Aquarium Drive. The parking lot is 0.1 mile on the right.*

2
Fairmount Park Houses

Distance: 12 miles

Difficulty: Easy

Terrain: Mostly flat with three moderate hills. The first 4 miles rise 100 feet before you descend quickly back to the river. You will then climb 200 feet above the river up to Belmont Plateau in 1.6 miles. Finally, George's Hill Road rises 100 feet in 0.5 mile. Suitable for any type of bicycle.

Location: The ride begins and ends at the Philadelphia Museum of Art at Eakins Oval and the Ben Franklin Parkway in Philadelphia. It is located 62 miles south of Allentown, 105 miles east of Harrisburg, 125 miles south of Scranton.

Of Special Interest: Many of the Fairmount houses are open to the public. Hours vary, but generally they are open 10–4 Monday through Friday. If you wish to visit, lock your bike, walk up to the front door, and knock. A caretaker or guide will admit you. A small admission fee may be charged.

Services: Lloyd Hall is the only concession on this route that is open daily; it sells snacks and beverages and has public toilets. In the summer, Edgely Ball Field has a food concession, which is open during ball field events.

To Get There

From I-76 or I-95, take I-676 exit. Take I-676 to the Ben Franklin Parkway exit. Follow signs to the Parkway and the art museum. Bear right at Eakins Oval and go straight on Kelly Drive, keeping the art museum on your left. A small traffic circle goes around a two-story statue of Abraham Lincoln in the middle of Kelly Drive. Go left, following the circle behind

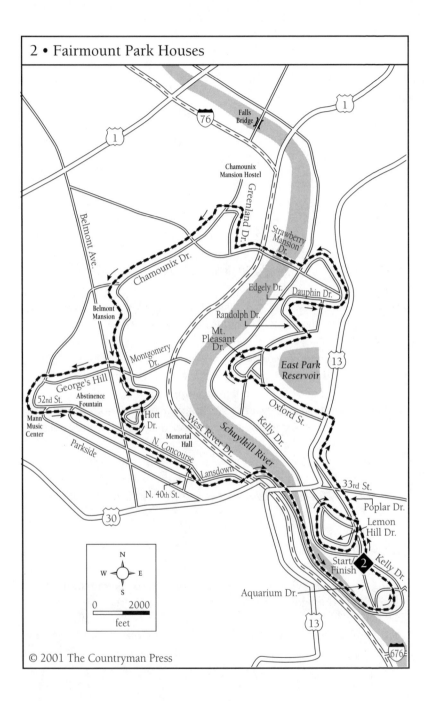

Falls Bridge

Chamounix Mansion Hostel

Greenland Dr.

Strawberry Mansion Dr.

Belmont Ave.

Chamounix Dr.

Edgely Dr.

Dauphin Dr.

Randolph Dr.

Belmont Mansion

Mt. Pleasant Dr.

East Park Reservoir

Montgomery Dr.

13

George's Hill

Oxford St.

52nd St.

Abstinence Fountain

Kelly Dr.

Mann Music Center

Hort Dr.

West River Dr.

Schuylkill River

Parkside

Memorial Hall

N. Concourse

Lansdown

33rd St.

Poplar Dr.

N. 40th St.

Lemon Hill Dr.

30

Start Finish

2

Kelly Dr.

N

W

E

S

Aquarium Dr.

0   2000

feet

13

676

© 2001 The Countryman Press

Lincoln. Continue on Aquarium Drive, straight ahead. The parking lot is in 0.1 mile on the right.

You could easily spend all day looking at the many historic houses and admiring the art on this ride. It travels from the art museum through the rolling hills on the east and west banks of the Schuylkill River. The hill where the museum is located was named "Faire Mount" by William Penn and has always been a park of some kind. In the early 18th century, residents came for picnics on the bluffs above the river and for walks through the woods.

The banks of the Schuylkill River were more accessible by the mid-1700s when the first roads were constructed. Wealthy residents bought the choice properties on top of the hills, which were desirable not only for their commanding views but also because the air in higher elevations was believed to be healthier.

Many original houses from this era survive and are part of Fairmount Park. This route passes several, including Lemon Hill, one of Philadelphia's first country estates. Early in the 19th century, the reservoir in Center City became inadequate to supply the growing population. A new one was created by pumping water from the Schuylkill River into an elevated reservoir on Fairmount. The Fairmount Waterworks were designed in neo-classical style, and the grounds were landscaped with pathways, gazebos, lawns, and sculpture, creating a 30-acre public park. The waterworks still exist, looking like a miniature of the art museum. However, they are no longer used and are closed to the public.

As the number of mills along the rivers and creeks increased, there was concern about pollution of drinking water. To prevent contamination of the Fairmount reservoir, the city purchased property along both banks of the river above the waterworks. In 1855, Lemon Hill's 45-acre formal gardens were purchased by the city and became a public garden. Fairmount Park was commissioned 12 years later and has grown steadily in size since then.

The Ride

0.0 Left on Aquarium Drive from the parking lot.

0.2 Cross Kelly Drive at the traffic circle around the Lincoln statue. Go straight on Poplar Drive.

0.3 Make a hard left on Lemon Hill Drive.

Pass Lemon Hill Mansion at 0.5 mile. In 1774, this was a 300-acre lemon orchard. The Federal-style house was erected in 1799, and 45 acres were converted to formal gardens, often called "the Versailles of America." A gazebo overlooking the river is on the left at 0.6 mile.

0.8 Right on Sedgley Drive.

1.0 Left on Poplar Drive.

1.3 Cross Girard Avenue at the traffic light where Poplar Drive becomes 33rd Street.

1.4 Straight to join US 13, still named 33rd Street.

1.8 Left at the traffic light on Oxford Street and enter East Fairmount Park.

2.3 Left on Mount Pleasant Drive.

2.4 Cross Fountain Green Drive. Go straight to stay on Mount Pleasant Drive.

2.5 Follow the road to the right around Mount Pleasant Mansion.

This is the most notorious of the Fairmount houses. Captain John MacPherson, a Scottish pirate, built it in the Georgian style in 1761. It was one of the most elegant and expensive country estates of its time.

Apparently, crime didn't pay, because MacPherson was forced to sell Mount Pleasant in 1779. The new owner, Benedict Arnold, purchased it for his bride. Unfortunately for the newlyweds, Arnold was accused of treason before they could move in.

At 2.6 miles, Rockland House, built in 1800, is on the left. This house is not open to the public.

2.8 Left at the stop sign on East Reservoir Drive, following the signs for East Park Tour.

This is a route designed for cars that passes many of the houses in the East Park. There is also a West Park Tour. Ormiston, 1798, is on the left at 2.9 miles. It is not open to the public.

3.1 Left on Randolph Drive, still following the East Park Tour signs.

Laurel Hill is at 3.3 miles. Built in 1748, it is one of the oldest remaining country estates. The original house is Georgian, but two wings were added in the early 19th century. The small one-story wing on the south side was added first. The octagonal wing was added later in an attempt to give the house a more modern appearance.

3.5 Edgely Ball Field is on the right.

A food concession is open here in the summer during ball field events.

3.7 Straight at the stop sign on Dauphin Drive, continuing to follow East Park Tour signs.

3.8 Left on Strawberry Mansion Drive before you reach the traffic light at US 13.

The Woodford Mansion, built in 1756 in Georgian style, is on the left and you will turn to pass in front of it. Woodford contains an excellent display of furniture and delftware china donated by Philadelphian Naomi Wood. Miss Wood owned one of the best private collections of 18th-century English-American household furnishings in the country. When she died, Woodford was chosen as the most appropriate site to display them.

3.9 Bear right on Strawberry Mansion Drive, continuing on the East Park Tour.

The original Strawberry Mansion, the largest of the Fairmount houses, was built in 1797 but was changed substantially over the next century. It is on your left at 4.1 miles.

4.4 Right on the Strawberry Mansion Bridge to cross the Schuylkill River.

After crossing the river, the road becomes Greenland Drive.

4.8 Bear right, continuing on Greenland Drive.

5.1 Bear left at the Y and turn left on Chamounix Drive.

5.4 Continue straight to stay on Chamounix Drive.

5.9 Continue straight on Chamounix Drive.

6.0 Left on Belmont Mansion Drive.

6.2 Belmont Mansion, 1755, is on the right, and a great view of the city skyline is on the left.

6.7 *Left through the gates on Horticulture Drive.*

6.9 *Pass the Horticultural Center and continue straight.*

The Pennsylvania Horticultural Society is the oldest horticultural organization in the United States. The Horticultural Society's demonstration gardens are on the right at 7.0 miles. In the middle stands *Night,* one of the first sculpture acquisitions of the Fairmount Park Art Commission.

7.2 *Follow the Park Tour signs to the left to ride around the Japanese House and Garden.*

The gardens are beautiful and worth at least peeking over the fence even if you don't have time to stop for a visit. The house and garden are open daily 11–4. Call 215-878-5097 for information.

7.4 *Double back and pass the Horticultural Center.*

7.8 *After exiting through the gates, turn right onto Belmont Mansion Drive.*

7.9 *Left on Montgomery Drive. Go straight across Belmont Avenue where Belmont Mansion Drive becomes Georges Hill Road.*

At the top of Georges Hill at 8.4 miles there is another nice view of the city.

8.5 *Left to stay on Georges Hill Road. Go down the hill to 52nd Street.*

8.7 *Straight through the traffic light on 52nd Street.*

The Mann Music Center is on the left.

8.9 *At the traffic circle, go around the Catholic Total Abstinence Union Fountain, continuing straight on North Concourse Drive.*

Memorial Hall is on the left at 9.5 miles. Philadelphia was chosen as the site for the Centennial Exposition of the United States in 1876. Both Memorial Hall and the abstinence fountain were built for the exposition. Memorial Hall was designed by Herman J. Schwartzmann and was an inspiration for many U.S. museums, including the Metropolitan Museum of Art in New York. It was one of the first American buildings to influence European architecture and was a model for the 1882 German Parliament building.

The design of the Smith Civil War Memorial was chosen from among 59 entries submitted in 1897. Thirteen artists collaborated on the final design.

9.8 Straight through the Smith Memorial Arch and continue straight on North 40th Street.

At the end of the 19th century, Philadelphia businessman Richard Smith bequeathed half a million dollars to design and construct a memorial to Civil War soldiers for Fairmount Park. The final plan was chosen from among more than fifty designs submitted by some of the best sculptors of the time. Thirteen artists contributed to the finished work.

9.9 Left on Lansdowne Drive at the stop sign.

10.2 Left at the 4-way stop onto Sweetbriar Road.

10.3 At the traffic light, cross West River Drive and turn right on the bike path.

Cross the Schuylkill River at 11.5 miles. From here you can see the Fairmount Waterworks. The buildings were designed with paved courtyards and walkways and a gallery where the public could view the machinery. Charles Dickens, who found most of the U.S. aesthetically and culturally disappointing, described the grounds surrounding the waterworks as the most beautiful he had ever seen.

11.6 When the bike path ends, cross the street in the crosswalk and get on the sidewalk/bike path that goes in front of the art museum.

Continue on the bike path with the museum on your left.

11.9 Go straight through the traffic lights at 25th Street and Fairmount Avenue.

12.1 Turn left on Aquarium Drive. The parking lot is 0.1 mile on the right.

3
The Drives

Distance: 28 miles
Difficulty: Easy
Terrain: Mostly flat with one climb. Andorra Road and Hart's Lane
climb 150 feet in 1.6 miles. Forbidden Drive is a 5.3-mile, wide,
gravel road, and the 2.3-mile towpath is unpaved and rough at times.
Unpaved bike paths make this ride more suitable for a mountain
bike or hybrid.
Location: The ride begins and ends at the Philadelphia Museum of Art
at Eakins Oval and the Ben Franklin Parkway in Philadelphia. It is
located 62 miles south of Allentown, 105 miles east of Harrisburg,
125 miles south of Scranton.
Services: Lloyd Hall, next to the parking lot on Aquarium Drive, sells
snacks and beverages and has public toilets.
Valley Green Inn (215-247-1730) has snacks and soft drinks.
There is also a formal dining room, but you should make reservations
ahead of time.
Bruno's Restaurant, at 11.0 miles, makes a great lunch stop. At
15.3 miles, just before the bicycle path, there is a small shop that
sells snacks.
Bicycle Shop: Metropolis Bicycles, 4159 Main Street; 215-508-5000.

To Get There

From I-76 or I-95, take I-676 exit. Take I-676 to the Ben Franklin Parkway exit. Follow signs to the Parkway and the art museum. Bear right at
Eakins Oval and go straight on Kelly Drive, keeping the art museum on
your left. A small traffic circle goes around a two-story statue of Abraham
Lincoln in the middle of Kelly Drive. Go left, following the circle behind

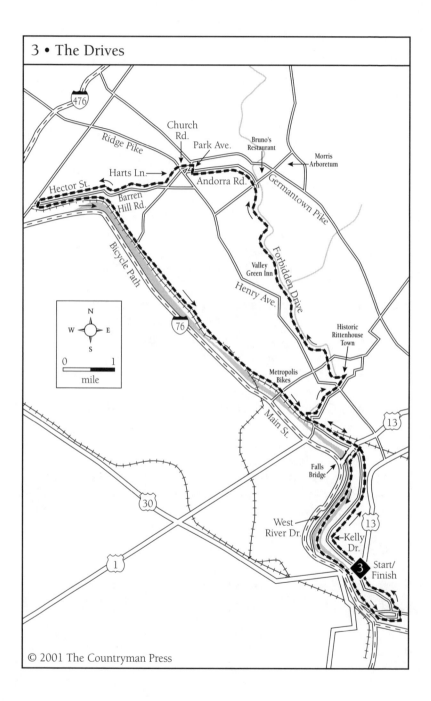

476

Ridge Pike

Church
Rd.

Park Ave.

Bruno's
Restaurant

Morris
Arboretum

Harts Ln.

Andorra Rd.

Hector St.

Barren
Hill Rd.

Germantown Pike

Bicycle Path

Forbidden Drive

Valley
Green Inn

N
W   E
S

76

Henry Ave.

0   1
mile

Historic
Rittenhouse
Town

Metropolis
Bikes

Main St.

13

Falls
Bridge

30

West
River Dr.

13

Kelly
Dr.

1

3 Start/
Finish

© 2001 The Countryman Press

Lincoln. Continue on Aquarium Drive, straight ahead. The parking lot is in 0.1 mile on the right.

This is a quiet, peaceful ride along some of Philadelphia's nicest bike paths. At 9,000 acres, Fairmount Park is the largest city park in the United States. It has expanded almost every year since it was created in 1867. The Fairmount Park Commission oversees many small parks scattered throughout Philadelphia, but the real gems are the banks of the Schuylkill River and Wissahickon Creek. There you can ride more than 40 miles from the Philadelphia Museum of Art to Valley Forge National Park and back along bicycle paths.

This ride follows the paths on both sides of the Schuylkill River, Wissahickon Creek, and the historic Schuylkill Canal Towpath. There is also a short section through the Main Street of Manayunk, where there are many interesting shops.

Freedom Valley Bicycle Trail in chapter 4 is a continuation of the bike route along the Schuylkill River and can be joined to this one if you want a longer ride.

For almost 200 years, hundreds of mills lined the river and creek banks. Responding to rising concerns about pollution and the loss of green spaces, the city purchased private and commercial land. Country estates were preserved for public use and commercial property was restored, resulting in the beautiful park that exists today.

In 1959, Philadelphia City Council passed a "percent ordinance" that required property owners and developers to provide public artwork equivalent to 1 percent of construction costs. The result of the ordinance is that, with over 200 individual works, Philadelphia has more public art than any other North American city.

The Ride

0.0 Left on Aquarium Drive from the parking lot.

0.1 Left on Kelly Drive bike path and pass Boathouse Row.

Rowing and sculling are popular sports on the Schuylkill River and there are many international regattas held here every year.

There are sculptures on both sides of Kelly Drive. On your right, don't miss *The Pilgrim* opposite Boathouse Row, *Cowboy* at 0.5 mile, or *Ulysses S. Grant* at 1.1 miles. On the left, opposite the statue of Grant, is my favorite piece, *The Playing Angels*.

Kelly Drive was named for John Kelly, a prominent Philadelphia businessman, Olympic rower, and father of Princess Grace of Monaco. There is a statue of him just after the reviewing stands at 1.6 miles. Whether it is affection, irreverence, or simply accessibility is debatable, but this sculpture is frequently "dressed" in various hats, scarves, and other miscellaneous apparel.

4.4 Where the bike path ends, turn left on the sidewalk on Ridge Avenue. Cross Wissahickon Creek.

4.5 Turn right at the light and cross Ridge Avenue.

There is a walk button at the traffic light to get you across this busy street. Go straight ahead onto the paved bike path. Hurricane Floyd turned the creek into a raging river in the summer of 1999. At this writing there was still one small section of the path in need of repair. It is open but unpaved for a few yards.

If you are ready for a break, continue straight on the Wissahickon path, passing Forbidden Drive, about 0.5 mile to Historic Rittenhouse Town. This is the site of the first paper mill in the United States, dating from 1690. While the houses are open to the public by appointment only, it is a nice place to stop, especially in the early spring when the cherry trees are in bloom.

5.8 Left on Forbidden Drive.

This wide, well-maintained gravel road is closed to motorized traffic. It follows Wissahickon Creek Gorge for 5.3 miles to the Philadelphia city limits.

It is hard to believe this quiet forest is in the heart of a big city. You will share the path with other cyclists, pedestrians, and perhaps a horse or two. The speed limit on Forbidden Drive is 7 mph. It is not enforced, but you should still keep your speed slow. Horses and pedestrians have the right of way, and remember that children are frequently unpredictable. Always give them plenty of room.

Visitors to the Wissahickon Gorge have been charmed for hun-

Forbidden Drive is a popular route for cyclists, walkers, joggers, and folks on horseback. The pace is leisurely, and everyone enjoys the scenery together.

dreds of years. The Leni-Lenape lived in the valley and hunted and fished along the creek. The name Wissahickon may come from the Lenape language. It is possible that it is from *wisamickan,* meaning "catfish," which are still abundant here. More likely, it is from *wissauchsikan,* meaning "yellow-colored stream."

The beauty and isolation attracted several religious groups. The Leni-Lenape are thought to have used the area for meetings and religious ceremonies. Johannes Kelpius and his followers arrived in 1695. Kelpius founded a religion called "The Society of the Woman of the Wilderness" who believed the end of the world would arrive near the end of the 17th century. They built a huge log cabin while Kelpius himself lived and prayed in a cave along the creek. They waited for the return of "the Woman" until Kelpius's death in 1708, when the group disbanded.

Early in the 18th century, Thomas Gorgas and his followers used the creek for baptisms into their independent Christian cult.

8.4 *Valley Green Inn (215-247-1730) is on the left.*

In the summer, snacks and soft drinks are sold from a window on the right side of the building. The restaurant is good but expensive. On summer weekends and evenings it is necessary to make a reservation.

11.0 *Left on paved Andorra Road at the end of Forbidden Drive.*

To the right, the road is Northwestern Avenue. Bruno's Restaurant, serving good, reasonable fare, is 1 block to the right. They are open from 6:30 AM to 9:30 PM every day except holidays.

Morris Arboretum is on the right, about 0.5 mile past Bruno's on Northwestern Avenue. It is open at least 10–4 every day and makes a pleasant place to spend an hour or two for a picnic lunch or wandering among the gardens. Admission is charged.

12.0 *Right at the end of Andorra Road on Park Avenue.*

12.1 *Left at the stop sign on Church Road.*

12.2 *Cross Ridge Avenue at the traffic light. The road becomes Hart's Lane.*

12.6 *Right on Barren Hills Road. Twist and turn along the road down to the river.*

13.8 *Bear right with the main road to stay on Barren Hills Road.*

14.0 *Left at the traffic light on Hector Street.*

15.3 *Left on Harry Street.*

15.4 *The entrance to the bicycle path is just past a small shop that sells cold drinks and snacks at the railroad tracks. Turn left and head toward Philadelphia.*

If you wish to take a longer ride, begin the Freedom Valley Bike Trail here.

18.9 *The bike path ends at Port Royal Road. Go right, down the hill less than 0.1 mile, and turn left on Nixon Street.*

19.2 *Go straight where Nixon Street ends and the historic Schuylkill Canal Towpath begins.*

Canals were an important method of transporting goods inland in the 19th century before the railroads. Mules walked along the paths, towing barges from one lock to another. This 5.3-mile trail was part of a network of canals that carried coal from the Pennsylvania highlands to the Delaware River, where it was loaded onto ships. This section of the bicycle path cannot be paved because the towpath is designated a National Historic Site. You will find the path rough at times.

21.5 Left at the end of the towpath.

21.5 Right on Main Street.

This is Manayunk, noted for many high quality restaurants and specialty boutique shops. Metropolis Bicycles is across the street. There is a good place for Italian ice on the left.

22.3 Continue straight where Main Street joins Ridge Avenue.

22.5 Pass the traffic light and cross Wissahickon Creek. Immediately after crossing the creek, turn right on Kelly Drive.

It is legal to ride in the street but you may feel more comfortable hopping back up on the bike path.

23.1 Right at the traffic light. Cross the river on the Falls Bridge.

23.3 Left on West River Drive bike path.

On weekends during the summer the road is closed to motorized traffic. Many cyclists, joggers, and skaters enjoy the wide, well-paved road.

27.3 Where the bike path ends after the river, cross the road in the crosswalk and get back on the bike path/sidewalk.

Continue straight. Follow the path all the way around, keeping the art museum on your left.

27.9 Left on Aquarium Drive, just before Boathouse Row. The parking lot is on the right in 0.1 mile.

II
VALLEY FORGE

Valley Forge

Valley Forge was the site of the winter quarters of the Continental Army in 1777–78. Twelve hundred men arrived on December 19 exhausted from several defeats including the British occupation of Philadelphia, the capital of the provisional government. By the end of December there were 6 inches of snow on the ground, and the Schuylkill River was frozen. Many men had no shoes and blankets were scarce. At times the only food was "firecake," plain flour mixed with water cooked over a campfire.

Several nearby farms and homes boarded the officers, but most of the soldiers did not even have tents when they arrived. Their first task was to build more than 1,000 wooden huts to shelter themselves from the freezing temperatures. You will see replicas of them along the route. Imagine one as the home to 10 or more men for six months.

The huts were warm, but they were damp. Air circulation was insufficient, and sanitation was poor. These conditions made the transmission of infectious diseases a serious problem. It is estimated that 2,000 soldiers died that winter from exposure, starvation, and disease. At one point, more than 4,000 were listed as too ill for duty.

The army also suffered from lack of training, experience, and cohesion. General George Washington, commander of the army, hired Baron Frederich von Stueben to train the men. Von Stueben had been a member of the King of Prussia's elite guard. Even though he spoke little English, he was a charismatic leader and a source of inspiration to the downtrodden troops. Through intense training and by personal example von Stueben renewed their faith in the cause.

As spring arrived with fair weather, new recruits, and fresh supplies, the men were ready to pursue the British who had left Philadelphia and were marching on New York. The war continued for five more years, but the triumph of spirit over suffering solidified the Continental Army's resolve to gain independence from Britain.

Linking Routes: The turn-around point of Freedom Valley Bike Trail is the starting point of Valley Forge National Park tour. If you combine these two routes, your ride will be about 47 miles.

Another alternative is to ride around Valley Forge National Park's Encampment Driving Tour. This 8-mile tour is clearly marked and easy to follow. Free maps are available in the visitor's center.

4

The Freedom Valley Bike Trail

Distance: *19 miles*
Difficulty: *Easy*
Terrain: *Mostly flat with one hill in Valley Forge National Park of 100 feet in 0.5 mile, and one climb on Old Eagle School Road of 375 feet in 2 miles. The entire route is paved. The bike path uses the railroad bed along the banks of the Schuylkill River. Suitable for any type of bicycle.*
Location: *Conshohocken, 15 miles west of Philadelphia, 60 miles south of Allentown, 90 miles east of Harrisburg, 130 miles south of Scranton.*
Services: *There is a small shop that sells snacks and beverages next to the bike path in Conshohocken. There are picnic areas and public toilets in the national park.*

Just before you finish the ride, there is a McDonald's restaurant and a WaWa convenience store in Conshohocken on the opposite side of the river from the bike path. To stop at one of them, turn right on Front Street from Matsonford Road at 19.0 miles, instead of crossing the river. Continue one block. McDonald's is on the right and the WaWa is straight ahead.

To Get There

Take I-76 to the Conshohocken exit. Follow signs to Conshohocken, bringing you to Front Street and Matsonford Road, which crosses the Schuylkill River. Go straight across the river. Turn at the first right on Elm Street. Turn right again at the next street, Harry Street. There is a parking area just before the railroad tracks. The bike path is next to the tracks. Take the bike path toward Valley Forge. Signs will point the way.

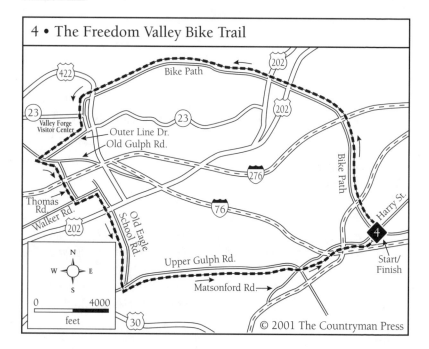

4 • The Freedom Valley Bike Trail

© 2001 The Countryman Press

The Delaware Valley Bicycle Coalition continues to improve cycling for everyone in the Greater Philadelphia area. They lobby for better signs, bike lanes, education, and transportation of bikes on public transit. Among their many accomplishments is facilitating the completion of a bike path from the Philadelphia Museum of Art to Valley Forge National Park.

The construction of the path was funded in part by proceeds from the coalition's annual Freedom Valley Bike Ride. Held in late May or early June, it includes rides from 8 to 70 miles in length, multiple food stops, and lots of fun.

This route follows the path from the Philadelphia suburb of Conshohocken, about 15 miles northwest of Center City, to Valley Forge. There, you will turn to the south and return to Conshohocken through some of the western suburbs.

The starting point for this ride is the turn-around point of chapter 3, The Drives, beginning from the art museum. If you combine the two routes, your ride will be about 47 miles.

The return route travels through Upper Merion, Tredyffrin, and Radnor Townships. These are more like small towns than suburbs, having a distinct character of their own.

The Ride

0.0 *Start on Harry Street and the bike path going toward Valley Forge.*

The path is flat, paved and popular with local cyclists, walkers, joggers, and skaters.

8.2 *Left toward Valley Forge National Park at the end of the bike trail. Cross the river on the pedestrian bridge next to US 422.*

If you are ready for a picnic break or want to do a bit of walking, don't cross the river yet. Continue straight on the bike path for 0.25 mile to the Betzwood picnic area. There are tables, a parking area, and public toilets. There is also a 2.5-mile walking trail along the Schuylkill River, accessible at the far left end of the parking area.

8.6 *Left on PA 23 at the stop sign.*

If you wish to stop at the visitors center, to take the auto tour or to continue on the Valley Forge National Park ride (chapter 5), follow the signs to the visitors center about 0.2 mile.

The forge that this area was named for was burned to the ground by British troops in 1777, several months before the Continental Army camped here.

8.8 *Right on Outer Line Drive.*

This was the position of the first line of defense during the Continental Army's winter encampment of 1777–78. The wood huts on the right are replicas of the ones the soldiers used. Each hut housed about 10 soldiers during their 6-month stay here.

10.0 *Left at the National Memorial Arch on Old Gulph Road.*

The arch was dedicated in 1917.

10.2 *Right on Thomas Road.*

You are now leaving the national park and will ride through some

The bike trail extends from the Philadelphia Museum of Art to Valley Forge National Park. The Bicycle Coalition of Delaware was instrumental in its construction.

of Philadelphia's western suburbs. This road is quiet and woodsy with scattered homes.

11.1 Left on Walker Road.

11.6 Right on Old Eagle School Road.

This is the only climb of this route. Old Eagle School brings you back into more populated settings.

13.7 Left on Upper Gulph Road.

Your route will be more downhill than uphill from here to Conshohocken.

17.4 Left on Matsonford Road. Continue straight to the river on Matsonford Road.

Don't let the number of roads converging here confuse you. Just keep going straight ahead.

19.0 Straight at the traffic light at Front Street onto the bridge.

Cross the river, unless you want to stop at the McDonald's restaurant or the WaWa convenience store. In that case, turn right on Front Street before the bridge. McDonald's is on the right and WaWa is straight ahead in 1 block. This store is a popular place for local riders to get snacks and cold drinks during long rides.

19.4 Right on Elm Street immediately after crossing the river.

19.4 Turn at the first right on Harry Street. The parking area is 0.1 mile ahead.

Linking Routes

The turn-around point of Freedom Valley Bike Trail is the starting point of Valley Forge National Park tour. If you combine these two routes, your ride will be about 47 miles.

Another alternative is to ride around Valley Forge National Park's Encampment Driving Tour. This 8-mile tour is clearly marked and easy to follow. Free maps are available in the visitor's center.

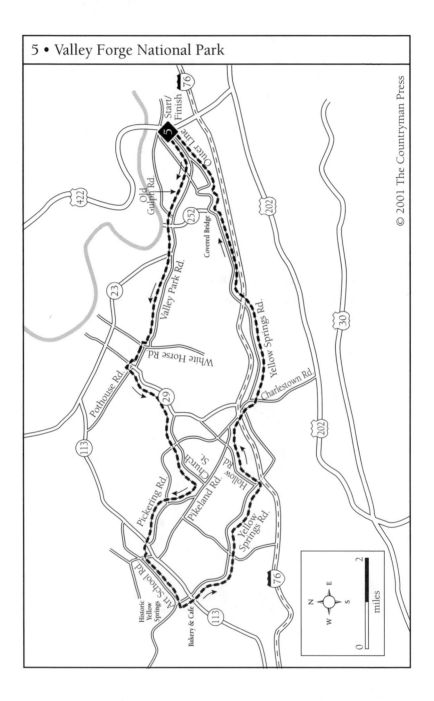

5
Valley Forge National Park

Distance: *30 miles*
Difficulty: *Moderate*
Terrain: *Moderately rolling to hilly, on paved roads or bike paths. You will encounter moderate traffic for 0.7 mile on PA 23 at 2.3 miles. A bicycle of any type is suitable provided it has several gears for climbing hills.*
Location: *Valley Forge National Park, 20 miles west of Philadelphia, 60 miles south of Allentown, 85 miles east of Harrisburg, and 130 miles south of Scranton.*
Of Special Interest: *Valley Forge is one of the most famous landmarks of the American Revolution. The park contains 3,600 acres of rolling hills with 6 miles of bike/foot trails and 10 miles of horse trails.*

The visitors center staff can help with overnight lodging and local restaurants and can answer questions about the park. During the summer, rangers conduct programs and tours. The map of the self-guided tour route is free. An 18-minute film, shown every 30 minutes in the visitors center, is also free. For more information, contact the Superintendent of Valley Forge National Park at P.O. Box 953, Valley Forge, PA 19482–0953.

Services: *There are three places to stop for food on the ride. The Valley Forge Corner Minimart is on the left at 3 miles on PA 23. Another country store is located at the T on Pickering Dam and Charlestown Roads at 8.5 miles. There are two small cafes and a bakery at 14.8 miles at the intersection of Yellow Springs Road and PA 113.*

Valley Forge National Park abuts a commercial district with two large shopping malls and several major hotels and convention centers.

There are many places to eat or to spend the night within 5 miles of the starting point. One of the least expensive is Motel 6, 815

North DeKalb Pike in King of Prussia; 610-265-7200. Valley Forge
B&B (610-933-6460) is about 2 miles past the intersection at PA 23
and Valley Park Road at 3.2 miles on the route. The address is 137
Forge Hill Road, Phoenixville, PA.

To Get There

Take I-76 to US 202. Go south on US 202 0.6 mile to US 422. Go north
1.6 miles and turn left on PA 23. Follow signs to the visitors center parking lot. The ride begins on the multi-use path between the parking lot
and the visitors center.

The ride begins in the national park along the first section of the
Encampment Trail. You will then follow Pickering Creek through sparsely developed wooded hills. You will pass through the renovated buildings of the 18th-century village of Yellow Springs, returning to the park
on country roads.

The Ride

0.0 *Start on the bike path between the parking lot and the visitors center, going up the short hill.*

0.2 *Follow the bike path to the right to Outer Line Drive following
the Encampment Auto Tour.*

On the right at 0.5 mile you can see replicas of soldiers' huts.
There were over 1,000 of these during the encampment, and each
one housed about 10 soldiers.

1.2 *At the Y, bear left to the stop sign. Cross the road and continue toward the National Memorial Arch.*

The arch was dedicated in 1917 to the "patience and fidelity" of
the Continental Army.

1.3 *Right on Old Gulph Road just before the arch.*

You will be on uneven Belgian blocks for a few yards before
returning to paved roads. There are many old streets in the
Philadelphia region that are still paved with Belgian blocks. These

stone cubes, measuring about 4 inches per side, were carried as ballast in ships crossing the Atlantic Ocean. The blocks were unloaded here and replaced with goods manufactured in the colonies to be sold in Europe.

2.5 Straight at the stop sign to join PA 23.

The next 0.7 mile is in moderate traffic, and the shoulder is poor. Take a deep breath, and remember you will be back on quiet, peaceful roads soon. The Valley Forge Country Minimart is on the left at 3.1 miles.

3.2 Left on Valley Park Road at the Valley Forge Baptist Church.

Valley Park Road has a rural, small-town feel as you roll past small, older homes.

3.6 Bear right at the stop sign to stay on Valley Park Road.

5.3 Right again to stay on Valley Park Road where Clothier Springs Road joins from the left.

5.6 Right on White Horse Road.

5.7 Left at the yellow flasher on Pot House Road immediately after crossing Pickering Creek.

This is a lovely, dark, and woodsy road.

6.3 Left on PA 29.

7.6 Bear right on Pickering Dam Road, leaving PA 29.

This picturesque road is quiet and hilly.

8.5 Right at the T on Charlestown Road.

There is a country store at this intersection.

8.6 Left on Church Street, another lovely road.

9.9 Right on Pikeland Road at the T.

Don't worry about that giant hill looming ahead. You'll turn before you get there, so just enjoy the view.

10.3 Right on Merlin Road.

11.2 Left at the first intersection on Pickering Road.

Do not cross the creek here.

12.0 Cross the creek on a one-lane bridge.

These are reproductions of the huts that each housed about ten soldiers for six months during the brutal winter of 1776.

12.3 Left at the T on Pine Springs Road, PA 113.

Traffic is fast on this road, but there are few cars, and there is a good shoulder.

12.6 Take the next right on Kimberton Road.

You are back into quiet, wooded, country roads.

12.8 Left at the T on Art School Road and immediately cross the creek.

14.3 Historic Yellow Springs is on the right.

These four 18th-century buildings were renovated as art galleries, antiques stores, and a restaurant. This was the site of a Revolutionary War hospital commissioned by the Continental Congress. It was later a Civil War orphans' school. Paths that wind through water gardens are open to the public.

14.3 Left on Yellow Springs Road.

14.8 Straight at PA 113 to stay on Yellow Springs Road.

A bakery and cafe are on the right. Enter onto PA 113. Yellow

Springs Road becomes wooded and sparsely populated again after crossing PA 113.

18.2 *Left on Hollow Road and climb up the hill.*

19.5 *Right at the T on Pikeland Road.*

20.0 *Right at the stop sign to join Charlestown Road.*

20.5 *Straight at the intersection with PA 29.*

21.2 *Left on Yellow Springs Road after passing under I-76.*

23.6 *Straight at North Valley Road to stay on Yellow Springs Road.*

23.7 *Straight to stay on Yellow Springs Road and leave the main road where North Diamond Hill Road joins from the left.*

26.4 *Follow the road to the right over the creek on the covered bridge.*

26.5 *Right on PA 252 and enter Valley Forge National Park.*

26.8 *Cross PA 252 on the bike path at Knox's Headquarters. Continue to follow the bike path on the left side of PA 252.*

30.0 *Follow the bike path to the left of the auditorium.*

30.2 *Left into the parking lot.*

Linking Routes

The turn-around point of Freedom Valley Bike Trail is the starting point of Valley Forge National Park tour. If you combine these 2 routes, your ride will be about 47 miles.

Another alternative is to ride around Valley Forge National Park's Encampment Driving Tour. This 8-mile tour is clearly marked and easy to follow. Free maps are available in the visitor's center.

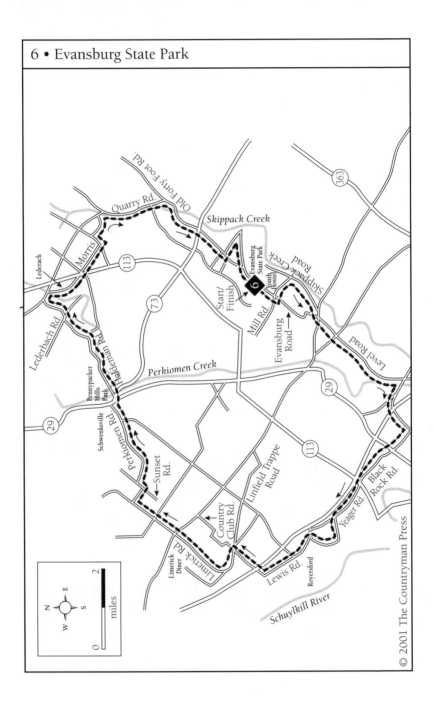

6
Evansburg State Park

Distance: *33 miles*

Difficulty: *Moderate*

Terrain: *Moderately rolling throughout. All roads are paved. Suitable for any bicycle.*

Location: *Evansburg State Park, in Montgomery County between Norristown and Collegeville. Twenty-five miles west of Philadelphia, 60 miles south of Allentown, 80 miles east of Harrisburg, 130 miles south of Scranton.*

Of Special Interest: *The Friedt Visitor Center at the Evansburg State Park Office has displays on flora and fauna in the area. You can take a self-guided walk along nearby Old Farmstead Trail, wander through the gardens, and participate in regularly scheduled programs on local history and ecology. There are ball fields, horse trails, and hiking paths that are accessible from many places within the park. The park office can provide information about all of these.*

Services: *Evansburg State Park has picnic areas and public toilets. The Evansburg State Park Youth Hostel is located within park boundaries at 837 May Hall Road, Collegeville, PA 19426; 610-489-4326. There is camping at French Creek State Park; see chapter 7 for details. Evansburg State Park is about 5 miles from Valley Forge National Park, the starting point for chapter 5. See that chapter for additional information on overnight lodging.*

Around 11 miles, you will enter the town of Royersford where there are several places to eat or to buy food and beverages. The Limerick Diner is on the left on West Ridge Pike at 16 miles.

To Get There

Take I-76 or I-276 to the Valley Forge exit. Go north on US 422 about 7 miles to PA 29, Collegeville Road. Go east, to the right on PA 29 into the town of Collegeville where PA 29 becomes Second Avenue. Turn right on Ridge Pike after about 2 miles. Stay on Ridge Pike where PA 29 turns left. Turn left on Evansburg Road after about 1 mile. The entrance to Evansburg State Park is to the right on Mill Road in about 1.5 miles. In 0.8 mile, follow signs on the left to May Hall Road. Park in the lot across the road from the youth hostel, on the right in about 0.7 mile.

Evansburg State Park is a welcome spot of undeveloped woods along Skippack Creek in the middle of suburban Philadelphia. Skippack Creek runs through a narrow valley first settled by Mennonites. By 1714, Skippack Pike connected the area to Philadelphia. You will ride near an eight-arch stone bridge built in 1792 that crosses Skippack Creek on Germantown Pike. It is one of the oldest bridges in continuous use in the country.

German immigrants built the state park's Friedt Visitor Center in the early 1700s. The same family owned and lived in the house for 190 years. There are herb gardens, a root cellar, and a well outside the house, maintained as they would have appeared in the 18th century.

The area was mostly farmland until after World War II, when the suburbs expanded into the valley. The land for the state park was acquired through "Project 70 Land Acquisition and Borrowing Act." The purpose of this act is to allow the state to buy land in areas of rapid development for the preservation of natural areas, open spaces, and parks, for use by all residents.

This route follows Skippack Creek for a while and then enters Royersford, one of Philadelphia's suburbs. Then, leaving new developments behind, you'll head out into farmland. Schwenksville is a picturesque little town on Perkiomen Creek. The term "exurb" is more descriptive of this area. There are still signs that civilization lurks somewhere close by, but the countryside is mostly open and undeveloped. You will pass a few Mennonite farms before Quarry Road takes you back to Skippack Creek and Evansburg State Park.

Please note that bicycles are allowed only on roads that are open to motorized traffic. Bikes are not allowed on hiking or horse trails.

Also be aware that hunting is allowed in season along Skippack Creek Road, miles 0.7 to 1.7. Check with park rangers if you ride here in the fall. Wear highly visible clothing, bright orange if possible, and it's not a bad idea to make some human-sounding noise as well.

The Ride

0.0 *Start in the Evansburg State Park parking lot, turning left on Mayhall Road.*

0.8 *Straight where Mayhall Road becomes Skippack Creek Road.*

This is a lovely quiet road with little or no traffic. The trees provide enough shade to make the ride pleasant here even on the hottest days.

1.8 *Right on Germantown Pike after a short, steep hill.*

The stone bridge that crosses Skippack Creek to your left is one of the oldest in the United States. This is a busy road, but there is a shoulder, and you will turn left at the light at the next intersection.

2.2 *Left on Evansburg Road.*

Note the 18th-century cemetery on your right at this intersection. You will climb gently as you ride through this quiet residential area.

3.4 *Straight where Evansburg Road becomes Level Road. Then downhill, back to Skippack Creek.*

4.6 *Right on Arcola Road. Cross Skippack Creek.*

4.7 *Right to stay on Arcola Road.*

5.1 *Left on Troutman Road.*

You can't miss this road; it's the one that goes up. This is the toughest hill on this ride. You will pass under US 422 at mile 5.4. You'll reach the summit in a newly developed residential area at about mile 5.8.

6.0 *Right on Black Rock Road. Enjoy a mostly downhill run for the next 3.5 miles.*

This area is changing rapidly from farmlands to suburbs.

7.8 *Go straight across PA 113 where Black Rock Road becomes Yeager Road.*

Those are the cooling towers of the Limerick Nuclear Reactor straight ahead of you. You'll get a better look a little later even though the ride turns before you reach them.

8.9 *Left on Mingo Road.*

This will bring you squarely into the suburbs. There are several expensive developments along this section of the ride.

9.7 *Bear right where Mingo Road becomes Thomas Road.*

When you reach Mingo Creek you will be at the bottom of the hill and will start to climb a bit.

9.9 *Bear right where Mingo Road becomes Vaughn Road.*

10.1 *Left on Lewis Road.*

11.0 *Enter Royersford.*

At the second traffic light, Main Street, there are many options for food and beverages.

11.6 *Right on Country Club Road. Pass over US 422 at 11.8 miles.*

Now you are in open farmland.

12.5 *Left on East Linfield Trappe Road at the stop sign.*

This is a very pretty road.

13.0 *Right on South Limerick Road.*

This is your best view of the Limerick cooling towers.

14.5 *Straight at the stop sign on West Ridge Pike to stay on Limerick Road.*

The Limerick Diner is to your left on Ridge Pike.

16.0 *Right to stay on Limerick Road at the stop sign. You will continue on the main road.*

16.5 *Left at the T on Sunset Road.*

16.7 *Follow the main road to rejoin Limerick Road.*

Sunset Road continues straight, but it is the smaller road.

18.6 *Follow the main road to the left where it becomes Perkiomen Road.*

These friendly donkeys live on Lederback Road. They'll come up to the fence for a chat if you have the time to stop and visit.

The road quickly turns to the right again, and you will soar down a 14 percent grade into the charming town of Schwenksville.

18.8 Right on PA 29, Main Street, at the T at the traffic light.

You might want to stop to look through the antique stores here.

19.0 Left on PA 73, Haldeman Road.

PA 29 is a busy road. Take your time crossing at this intersection with no traffic light. Cross over the Perkiomen Creek heading toward Skippack.

19.2 Left to stay on Haldeman Road immediately after crossing Perkiomen Creek and enter the Perkiomen Watershed Conservancy.

You will leave the main road here, which will continue as PA 73. Pennypacker Mills Park is on the left. George Washington used the Pennypacker Mill as his headquarters in September and October of 1777. This was also the last home of Samuel W. Pennypacker, governor of Pennsylvania from 1903 to 1907. He died here on

September 16, 1916. This area is still very rural, and there are many farms among the rolling hills.

20.5 Left to stay on Haldeman Road at the T.

21.4 Right on Lederbach Road at the T at the stop sign.

Some very friendly donkeys live near this intersection. If they are out when you pass by, they'll like it if you to stop to scratch them on the nose.

21.6 Take the next left on Haldeman Road.

You leave the main road here. The sign is hard to see, so just turn at the next road. Lederach Road becomes Camp WaWa Road here. You will ride downhill to the East Branch of Perkiomen Creek. On your way you'll have a great view of a lovely Mennonite farm.

22.3 Cross the small creek at the bottom.

After passing the farm, turn right at the stop sign on Salfordville Road. You will cross Perkiomen Creek and enter the village of Lederach.

23.5 Go straight across PA 113 where Salfordville Road becomes Morris Road.

Day Pony Inn and Old Skippack Inn are at this intersection. You have also reached the top of the hill.

24.2 Turn left to continue on Morris Road.

You will still follow the main road here.

24.4 Right to stay on Morris Road at the T where the stop sign reads STOP EXCEPT RIGHT TURN.

25.2 Right on Quarry Road. Following Quarry Road, which is the main road, bear left and then quickly turn right, crossing a small creek at 26.0 miles.

26.7 Cross Skippack Creek on a lovely old bridge.

26.8 Right on Old Forty Foot Road at the T.

27.1 Bear right to stay on Old Forty Foot Road.

27.3 Bear left to stay on Old Forty Foot Road.

28.0 Cross Skippack Pike, PA 73, where the road becomes Evansburg Road.

28.8 Left on Kratz Road.

29.3 Right on Anders Road.

30.2 Left on Evansburg Road.

31.2 Left on Mill Road following signs for Evansburg State Park.

31.8 Left on May Hall Road following signs for the park office.

The parking lot is 0.7 mile ahead on the right.

7 • French Creek State Park and Hopewell Furnace National Historic Site

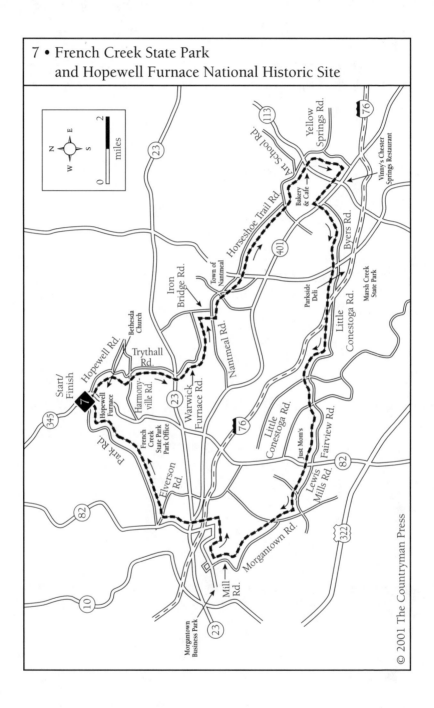

© 2001 The Countryman Press

7

French Creek State Park and
Hopewell Furnace National Historic Site

Distance: *49 miles*

Difficulty: *Moderate to Difficult*

Terrain: *Hilly. All roads are paved with 0.9 mile of light gravel on Piersoll Road, mile 1.5. Suitable for any bike.*

Location: *Hopewell Furnace National Historic Site, 45 miles northwest of Philadelphia, 60 miles southwest of Allentown, 65 miles east of Harrisburg, 100 miles south of Scranton.*

Of Special Interest: *Hopewell Furnace National Historic Site is restored to its 1830 appearance, including a cold-blast furnace and functioning water wheel. The ironmaster's mansion, the company store, workers' homes, and a blacksmith shop are restored and open to the public. During the summer, there are regular programs led by costumed guides. Hopewell Furnace is open daily 9–5. For more information: Hopewell Furnace National Historic Site, 2 Mark Bird Lane, Elverson, PA 19520; 610-582-8773.*

You will have a chance to visit Marsh Creek State Park at 23 miles. Marsh Creek Lake is a popular spot for small-boat sailing, canoeing, and fishing. There is a picnic area and a 6-mile trail system. The swimming pool is open 11–7 daily in the summer. There is also a concession stand serving food and beverages.

With over 7,000 acres, French Creek has ample space for many outdoor pastimes. There are more than 32 miles of hiking trails; maps are available at the park office. Several organized nature and interpretive walks with rangers are scheduled during the summer.

Licensed hunting and fishing are also permitted in the park in season.

Services: *French Creek State Park (610-582-9680) has 201 campsites. The south entrance is about 1.5 miles south of Hopewell Furnace on*

PA 345. Campsites are open all year. Reservations may be needed for weekends during the summer. The state park also has 10 cabins with heat, electricity, bathrooms, and cooking facilities. You will definitely want reservations for cabins.

A youth hostel with 12 beds operates within the boundaries of Marsh Creek State Park. Contact Marsh Creek Hostel, East Reeds Road, Box 376, Lyndell, PA 19354; 610-458-5881.

There is a bakery and cafe in the Shops at Pickering Mills on Yellow Springs Road and PA 113 at 14.7 miles. Vinny's Chester Springs Restaurant and a small market are at 17.6 miles at the intersection of PA 113 and PA 410. Parkside Deli and Pizza is located at Little Conestoga and Park Roads at 21 miles. Marsh Creek State Park operates a food concession near the park office at 23 miles. Just Mom's serves snacks at 32.4 miles to the right on PA 82. There is a general store on PA 345, a few miles south of Hopewell Furnace.

To Get There

Take exit 22 of I-76, Morgantown interchange. Follow PA 10 South to PA 23 East. After about 4.5 miles on PA 23 East, take PA 345 North. Follow signs for about 4 miles to the Hopewell Furnace National Historic Site. Turn left to reach the parking area.

Ironmaster Mark Bird founded Hopewell Furnace in 1771. Bird chose this spot because of its proximity to raw materials such as charcoal and iron ore, and to roads linking the furnace to markets. The giant bellows that provided air for the fire were powered by water flowing through French Creek.

The furnace produced cannon, shot, and shell for the American Revolution. In the following years, workers made pots, kettles, machinery, and grates, reaching peak production from 1820 to 1840. Hopewell Furnace workers made the doors for the Eastern State Penitentiary in 1826 and 1827. But the most profitable products were coal- and wood-burning stoves. The furnace closed in 1883.

Until it closed, providing charcoal for the furnace was the principal local industry. You can still find the remains of charcoal hearths scattered through the woods in French Creek State Park.

Warwick Furnace Road is one of the most
picturesque cycling routes in the area.

Land was originally acquired for the park and historic site in 1934 as part of the Civilian Conservation Corps (CCC) and the Works Progress Administration (WPA), federal programs designed to help ease unemployment during the Great Depression. Thousands of unemployed young men were hired by the government and trained by retired military officers and conservationists. The programs provided marketable skills and work experience for the young men, and created parks and maintained natural areas for public use. In 1946 the land was turned over to the Commonwealth of Pennsylvania.

The Ride

0.0 Begin in the parking lot for Hopewell Furnace National Historic Site. Cross PA 342 and go straight on Hopewell Road.

At 1 mile, you will pass Bethesda Road, where Bethesda Church and Cemetery are set back a few hundred feet. The building was originally a meetinghouse and was converted to a Baptist church in 1807. Workers at Hopewell Furnace attended the services.

1.5 Right on Piersol Road.

This road is paved but has a light covering of gravel in spots. The area is heavily wooded with a few older houses scattered along the way.

2.4 Left on Harmonyville Road at the stop sign at the T.

2.6 Right on Trythall Road.

You will cross French Creek at 2.7 miles, so named because a fort on the creek was occupied by the French during the French and Indian War, 1754–63.

4.1 Right on PA 23 at the stop sign.

4.3 Next left on Warwick Furnace Road.

The historic marker at this intersection states that in 1742 Anna Nut and Company made the first Franklin stoves. They also provided shot for American troops during the Revolutionary War.

Warwick Furnace Road starts with manicured lawns and well-kept houses. As you continue, the woods creep back in around older houses and small farms. This quiet, narrow, paved road turns back and forth a bit through here. Follow the main road and the traffic arrows.

7.1 At the stop sign, continue straight and then follow Warwick Furnace Road to the right, over a one-lane bridge. Immediately after the bridge, go straight on Iron Bridge Road.

Warwick Furnace Road turns to the left. Iron Bridge Road takes you even farther into the woods.

7.8 Left on Nantmeal Road at the stop sign and T.

8.4 Right on Coventry Road at the next stop sign.

8.5 Go straight at the stop sign.

Fairview Road comes first from the left and then from the right a few yards ahead. Continue straight on Coventry Road.

8.6 Continue straight on Horseshoe Trail Road at the stop sign where the main road turns right.

11.6 Cross PA 100.

Horseshoe Trail continues just slightly to the right on the other side of PA 100. Horseshoe Trail remains very rural here. As you continue, you will see a few more houses, some quite new and others that have been around a long time.

12.7 Left on Art School Road.

To the right is Chester Springs Road. This is another lovely little road through the woods. There are more older houses.

14.2 Right on Yellow Springs Road.

Historic Yellow Springs is a collection of renovated buildings dating to an 18th-century village. Here, the ride overlaps the Valley Forge National Military Park route at 14.3 miles.

14.7 Cross PA 113, continuing on Yellow Springs Road.

To the right on PA 113 you will find a bakery and small cafe in the Shops at Pickering Mill. Enter from PA 113. Yellow Springs Road continues on the other side of PA 113, bearing sharply to the left and going downhill.

15.6 Right on Pine Creek Road and continue to follow the creek.

The homes along this road are old, or made to look old. They are large properties with beautiful landscaping that makes good use of the creek.

15.9 Bear left to continue on Lower Pine Creek Road at the Y.

There is a road sign for Lower Pine Creek Road and a hand-painted sign for Horseshoe Trail to the right.

16.7 Right on PA 401.

17.6 Cross PA 113.

There is a minimart and a restaurant, Vinny's at Chester Springs. Vinny's serves breakfast, lunch, and dinner.

18.4 Left on Byers Road.

Once again, you will be riding next to manicured lawns and well-kept houses.

19.3 Continue on Byers Road, bearing right to stay on the main road.

19.8 Continue on Byers Road, bearing right to stay on the main road.

20.9 Right on PA 100, Pottstown Pike. PA 100 is a busy road. Stay close to the right side.

21.0 Left to cross PA 100 onto Little Conestoga Road after a few hundred yards.

There is a small market on the left and the Parkside Deli is on the right, just before you get to the traffic light at Park Road.

21.1 Turn left on Park Road to visit Marsh Creek State Park.

There is a swimming pool, food and beverage concessions, and lake and hiking trails. If you don't want to stop, keep going straight on Little Conestoga Road. It is 3.9 miles from here to the park office and back, so you will need to subtract that from the ride directions to match your bike computer.

23.1 Continue straight past the park office.

Mileage will be measured from this point. Keep that in mind if you want to cruise around a bit.

25.0 Left on Little Conestoga Road.

The road is lined with houses, many very recently built. There is every indication that building will continue in this area.

27.6 Left to stay on Little Conestoga Road at the T.

Styers Road is on the right. The traffic arrow points to the left.

28.0 Right to stay on Little Conestoga Road at Chalfont and Marshall Roads.

You have a stop sign, as does traffic from Chalfont Road, to the left. There is no stop for Marshall Road, straight ahead.

29.2 Left on Fairview Road at the stop sign.

You will see Fairview Presbyterian Church well before you get to the intersection.

32.4 A left followed by a quick right at the stop sign at PA 82, Manor Road.

The quick right will put you on Lewis Mills Road. This area is rural, with widely spaced farmhouses.

33.4 *Bear left at the Y to stay on Lewis Road at Wyebrook Road. Cross Brandywine Creek on Glen Cable Bridge and go up the hill to the stop sign.*

This is a very pretty area.

33.6 *Left on Creek Road.*

34.4 *First right on Chestnut Tree Road at the stop sign. There is no road sign.*

35.3 *Left on Morgantown Road almost to the top of a short, steep hill.*

You are entering another area of recent development.

37.7 *The road takes a hard turn to the right and becomes Mill Road.*

After about 0.5 mile, the land opens up onto some great vistas over the farmland. You won't see a road sign for Mill Road until 38.8 miles.

38.9 *Bear right at Best Road to stay on Mill Road.*

39.0 *Right on Valley Road.*

39.2 *Right at the Morgantown Business Park.*

This is Timber Road, but there are no signs until you turn onto Hemlock Road.

39.3 *Left on Hemlock Road at the stop sign.*

40.8 *Left on Twin Valley Road at the stop sign and exit the business park. Cross I-76 on an overpass at 41.0 miles.*

41.4 *Cross PA 23, Main Street at the traffic light.*

This light is triggered electronically by cars on Twin Valley Road. It will not detect you and your bike, so you will need to cross as if at a stop sign if there are no cars with you on Twin Valley Road.

42.8 *Right on Elverson Road, PA 82.*

42.9 *Bear left at the next Y onto Hopewell Road.*

The south entrance to French Creek State Park is on the right at 46.4 miles. Continue straight on Hopewell Road although a sign points to the right for Hopewell Furnace National Historic Site.

The park office and day-use parking lot is at 46.5 miles.

48.6 Right at the stop sign on PA 345.

49.2 Right into the Hopewell Furnace National Historic Site.

The parking area is 0.2 mile ahead.

Alternative routes

This ride overlaps the Valley Forge National Military Park ride at mile 14.2 on this ride and mile 14.3 on the Valley Forge route. You can take two or three days to complete both routes, stopping for the night in the Marsh Creek Hostel and the French Creek campground.

For a three-day ride, begin in the parking lot next to the visitors center at Valley Forge and ride to Yellow Springs Road, 14.3 miles. Switch to the French Creek ride at 14.2 miles and continue to the Marsh Creek Hostel; your distance for the day will be 23 miles. The next day you will follow the French Creek route and arrive in French Creek State Park at 25 miles. Your third day is a 30-mile ride from French Creek State Park to Yellow Springs Road. There, switch back to the Valley Forge route and ride back to the Valley Forge visitors center.

To take a two-day trip, consider starting from the parking area of the Shops at Pickering Mills. This is where the bakery and cafe are located on PA 113 and Yellow Springs Road, on the French Creek ride at 14.7 miles and at 14.8 miles on the Valley Forge route. Take the Valley Forge route to Valley Forge and then back out to the Shops at Pickering Mills. Then continue on to the hostel at Marsh Creek following the French Creek ride. This is about 37 miles. The next day, continue to French Creek State Park and on to Yellow Springs Road and the Shops at Pickering Mills, about 41 miles.

III
THE BRANDYWINE RIVER VALLEY

The Brandywine River Valley

In 1777, 12,000 British and Hessian troops under the command of Generals Howe, Cornwallis, and Knyphausen landed at the north end of the Chesapeake Bay, intent on capturing Philadelphia, seat of the Continental Congress. At 4 AM on September 9, in sweltering heat and humidity, they began a 17-mile march from Kennett Square to Brandywine Creek.

General George Washington and the Continental Army prepared to meet British troops, confident that they could stop them. Washington knew of three fords across the creek. He posted guards at the southern and northern positions, hoping to force the British across at Chadds Ford, where Washington felt he had the advantage.

However, General Howe knew of another ford north of the others. Howe sent 4,000 Hessian troops, commanded by Knyphausen, along the Great Road, now US 1. The plan was to create as much noise and smoke as possible and to meet and distract Washington while the rest of the British troops crossed to the north.

Around 9 AM, Continental troops, assigned as scouts to warn Washington when the British were near, were drinking in a tavern east of the Brandywine. The humidity created a dense fog, and the scouts did not see the approaching British troops until they were only about 100 yards away. The Continental scouts were so startled that they fired on the British from the tavern. There is no record of the reactions of other patrons. The scouts ran down the Great Road, forgetting their horses at the tavern.

Washington received conflicting reports about how many troops were approaching. One scout reported that there were thousands of troops—the bulk of Howe's army—heading north. But Washington decided to keep his troops intact at Chadds Ford. By the time he realized his mistake, the British were marching up behind the Americans.

The British won the battle decisively, but fighting was fierce and both sides suffered heavy casualties. The exhausted Americans retreated to the west, but the British did not have the strength to pursue them. Instead, they camped for the night before marching to Philadelphia.

These two rides take you through and around the Brandywine Valley. Although the Brandywine is officially named and classified as a creek, locals frequently refer to it as the Brandywine River. Don't let it confuse you; they are one and the same.

8
Brandywine Creek

Distance: 14 miles

Difficulty: Easy

Terrain: Paved with two hills. Miles 1.5 to 2.3 climb 100 feet up Allerton Road and Telegraph Road climbs 100 feet in 2 miles from 4.8 to 7.2 miles. Suitable for any bicycle.

Location: Brandywine Picnic Park at the intersection of PA 100 and PA 52. Twenty-five miles west of Philadelphia, 65 miles south of Allentown, 80 miles east of Harrisburg, 130 miles south of Scranton.

Of Special Interest: Longwood Gardens is 4 miles south of this route's starting point on PA 52. Longwood covers more than 1,000 acres of lawns, greenhouses, and formal and informal gardens. Leni-Lenape Indians lived here before European immigrants began farming the area in the late 17th century. In 1700, the Pierce family built the house that is still on the grounds. It has been renovated and features period furniture and a museum recounting the history of the grounds going back to the Leni-Lenape. The gardens are open year-round from at least 10–5. Admission is charged.

The Brandywine Tourist Information Center is next to Longwood Gardens on US 1 and PA 52 north.

If you travel 4 miles from the ride's starting point, south on PA 100, you will arrive at the Brandywine River Museum. This art gallery features the Wyeth family's paintings as well as those of many other American artists. Jamie, N. C., and Andrew Wyeth have lived and painted in this part of Pennsylvania for many years, drawing inspiration from the idyllic scenery.

Rental canoes are available on the Brandywine Creek at Northbrook Canoe Company (610-793-2279), 2 miles off the route at 9.5 miles. The Brandywine Scenic Railroad is next door.

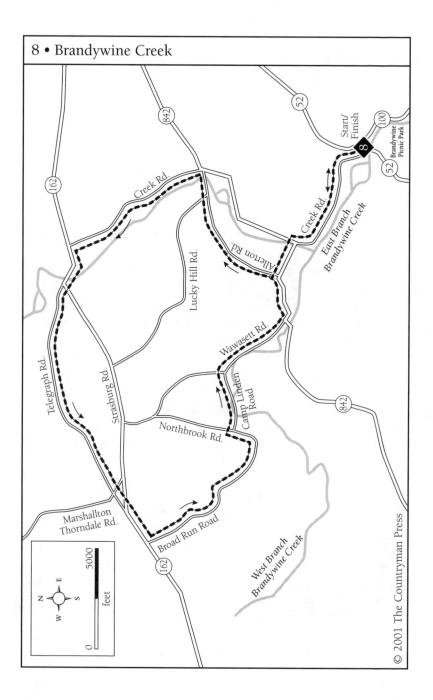

© 2001 The Countryman Press

Services: *There are public toilets at the Brandywine Picnic Park. There are no other services on this route. Chadds Ford is 4 miles south of Brandywine Picnic Park on PA 100. There is a hotel, convenience store, and a restaurant at the intersection of US 1 and PA 100. Hank's Place serves good quality diner-style food at reasonable prices. The phone number for the Brandywine River Hotel is 610-388-1200.*

For overnight lodging, there are several choices around Chadds Ford. You may also want to consider the 1810 House of Marshallton (610-430-6013) which is within a mile of the route at 1280 West Strasburg Road (PA 162) at around 5 miles. Whitewing Farm B&B is 3 miles south of the picnic park on PA 52. The address is 370 Valley Road, West Chester, PA 19382; 610-388-2665. For camping, 7 miles southwest is the Philadelphia West Chester KOA in Unionville. The address is P.O. Box 920, Unionville, PA 19375; 610-486-0447.

Bicycle Shop: *West Chester Bicycle Center, 1342 West Chester Pike; 610-431-1856, is about 3.5 miles north of the Brandywine Picnic Park on PA 100/52.*

To Get There

From the north or east, take I-76 to I-476 South. Exit on U.S. 1 South. At Chadds Ford, follow PA 100 to PA 52. Just before the intersection, turn left into the parking lot for the Brandywine Picnic Park.

From the west, take I-76 or U.S. 1 to PA 100. Follow PA 100 South to PA 52. Immediately after the intersection, turn right into the parking lot for the Brandywine Picnic Park.

This is a tranquil ride past fords the British troops used, through the gently rolling hills and farmland of Chester County. You will begin 1.4 miles south of where the Brandywine divides into east and west branches. Scenery varies from the deeply wooded Allerton Road, through the affluent suburbs along Telegraph Road, and then back along the West Branch through rolling farmland and horse country.

The Ride

0.0 Start in the parking lot of the Brandywine Picnic Park. Left on PA 100. PA 100 is joined by PA 52 at the first intersection.

0.3 Left on Creek Road immediately after the Delacy Soccer Park.

1.4 Left, crossing the East Branch of the Brandywine Creek on PA 842, Bridge Road.

1.8 Right on Allerton Road.

You will work a bit by climbing uphill to earn the pretty country scenery of this little road.

3.0 Right on Lucky Hill Road.

This hill is lucky for you because you will be going down.

Cross the East Branch of the Brandywine Creek. This was the location of Jeffrie's Ford, where British troops crossed the Brandywine. From here, they marched southwest for 4.5 miles to Osborne Hill, where they first engaged George Washington's troops.

3.2 Left on Creek Road immediately after crossing the creek.

4.8 Left on PA 162, Strasburg Road.

5.2 Right on Telegraph Road immediately after crossing the West Branch of the Brandywine Creek.

This area, lying a short distance from the towns of West Chester and Downingtown, is more suburban than rural.

7.4 Straight to join PA 162.

7.9 Left on Broad Run Road.

Now you are back in the country.

9.5 Left on Northbrook Road.

General Cornwallis and the British troops marched along this road from Kennett Square and made their first ford of Brandywine Creek, 2 miles south of here.

Just past that crossing, where a bridge replaces the ford, you will find Northbrook Canoe and the Scenic Brandywine Railroad.

9.8 Right on Camp Linden Road.

The Philadelphia Ethical Society is on the left. You are still biking on the trail used by the British troops.

10.4 Right on Wawasett (pronounced wah-WAH-set) Road.

The soldiers turned left here to follow a road that no longer exists, taking them over Lucky Hill and back down to Jeffrie's Ford. You will take a flatter route to the creek.

11.3 Straight to join PA 842.

Here you will retrace your route back to the start.

12.1 Right on Creek Road.

13.2 Right on PA 52.

13.5 Where PA 52 and PA 100 split, go straight on PA 100.

13.6 Right into the picnic park.

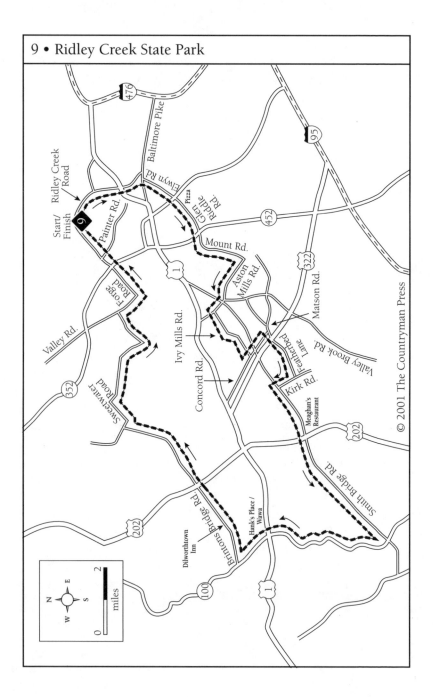

© 2001 The Countryman Press

9
Ridley Creek State Park

Distance: *37 miles*

Difficulty: *Moderate to Difficult*

Terrain: *Hilly throughout the route. All roads and the bike path are paved. Bicycles with several gears for hills are suitable.*

Location: *Ridley Creek State Park, 16 miles west of Philadelphia, 60 miles south of Allentown, 90 miles east of Harrisburg, 130 miles south of Scranton.*

Of Special Interest: *You will begin next to Tyler Arboretum (610-566-9134), a 654-acre nonprofit educational institution. In 1681, Thomas Minshall, an English Quaker, purchased the grounds from William Penn. Eight generations of the family lived here until 1944 when Laura Tyler, Minshall's direct descendent, bequeathed the property as a public arboretum. It is open daily from 8 AM until dusk. Admission is charged.*

Brandywine Battlefield Park is 1 mile to the right at 22.4 miles. Unfortunately, you may only enter the park via US 1, not a great bicycle route. However, if you are comfortable with heavy traffic (there is a good shoulder) or if you wish to drive, consider a visit. The grounds and museum are free. Two historic houses, Washington's and Lafayette's headquarters, are also located in the park. There is an admission fee for them.

Newlin Grist Mill Park (610-459-2359) is 1 mile off of the route at 10.3 miles. To reach it, instead of turning right, turn left on Concord Road. After 0.5 mile, turn right again on Cheyney Road. The Newlin Grist Mill Park is on the left in 0.5 mile. The park specializes in programs for children that teach about colonial life. Admission is charged.

Services: *The Elwyn station of Southeastern Pennsylvania Transit Association (SEPTA) regional rail R3 is on this route at 3.3 miles.*

There is a pizza place and pharmacy at 3.7 miles on PA 352. Meghan's Restaurant, serving breakfast and lunch, is at 13.9 miles just before you cross US 202. At the intersection of US 1 and PA 101 at 25.2 miles, there is a WaWa convenience store, a post office, and Hank's Restaurant.

The Brandywine River Hotel (610-388-1200) is also located at the intersection of US 1 and PA 100 in Chadds Ford. If you are looking for a campsite, the Philadelphia West Chester KOA is in Unionville, about 20 miles from the starting point in Ridley Creek State Park.

Bicycle Shop: *The West Chester Bicycle Center is located at 1342 West Chester Pike, West Chester, PA; 610-431-1856. It is about 10 miles west of the starting point in Ridley Creek State Park.*

To Get There

Take I-76 to I-476 South. Exit on US 1 South. Turn right on Providence Road. After 1 mile, turn left on Chapel Hill Road. At 0.5 mile, at the intersection with Ridley Creek Road, go straight and cross Ridley Creek. Park in the lot on the right.

On this route you will pass through Chadds Ford, where the Battle of the Brandywine started with a British deception. The intersection where the original ford was located is now the site of museums and other historic buildings.

The ride begins in Ridley Creek State Park near the remains of a small 18th century village that developed around two mills along the creek. Several buildings still exist.

Ridley Creek State Park also includes Colonial Pennsylvania Plantation. The plantation has been a working farm for more than 300 years and is now restored to its 18th-century appearance. There are regular programs on weekends between April and November with costumed guides giving demonstrations of 18th-century skills and chores.

The park, totaling over 2,000 acres, also includes a 5-mile bike/walk path, the last leg of this ride. There is a horse trail as well as 12 miles of hiking paths. Some of these connect to Tyler Arboretum, which is next to the park.

The Ride

0.0 Start at the parking lot at Barren Road and Forge Trail. Cross Ridley Creek on Chapel Hill Road.

0.0 Immediately after crossing the creek, turn right on Ridley Creek Road.

0.9 Turn right to stay on Ridley Creek Road at Sycamore Mills Road.

2.4 Right on Baltimore Pike.

This can be busy at times, but there is a shoulder and you will leave it for quieter cycling in 0.2 mile.

2.6 Left on Elwyn Road immediately after crossing the creek.

The Elwyn station of SEPTA regional rail line R3 is on this road.

3.6 Left on New Middletown Road, PA 352.

After you cross the creek, there is a pharmacy and a pizza restaurant on the right, just before the turn on Glen Riddle Road.

3.7 Right on Glen Riddle Road. Cross PA 452 at 5.0 miles.

5.5 Hard left to cross the creek on MacIntyre Drive.

There is no signpost for MacIntyre Drive, but it is the road that crosses Chester Creek. This is a very interesting old neighborhood with tiny homes stacked against each other along Lundgren Road, to your right.

5.6 Bear right on Team Road after the creek.

5.8 Bear right at the T on Mount Road and immediately go straight at the island on New Road.

6.8 Right at the stop sign on Aston Mills Road. Aston Mills Road becomes Birney Highway at 7.3 miles and then Llewelyn Road at 7.6 miles.

There are many new homes here, mixing with the old farmhouses.

8.1 Right at the T on PA 261, Valley Brook Road.

There is a firehouse on the right just before the stop sign.

8.6 Left on Ivy Mills Road at the top of the hill.

9.1 Continue on Ivy Mills Road as it bends to the left and Pole Cat Road comes in from the right.

Ridley Creek State Park contains a working 18th-century
plantation and a network of hiking trails.

You are back in the country in a pretty, wooded area.

10.3 Left at the stop sign on Concord Road, State Road (SSR) 3007.

10.5 Continue straight at the stop sign and flashing red light at Smith Bridge Road.

If you wish to visit the Newlin Grist Mill, turn right here. Continue for 0.5 mile and turn right on Cheyney Road. The park is on the left in 0.5 mile.

11.1 Right on Mattson Road just before Concord Road turns to the left.

11.3 Go straight across PA 322 at the stop sign.

On the other side, the road is Featherbed Lane.

12.5 Right on Kirk Road.

13.2 Left on Smith Bridge Road at the stop sign. Go straight across northbound US 202 at the traffic light at 14.6 miles.

Meghan's Restaurant is on the right, serving breakfast and lunch from 6:30 AM to 2 PM. Cross southbound US 202 southbound at the next traffic light at 14.7 miles.

18.5 Right on PA 100 at the 4-way stop sign. The intersection is not marked.

22.4 Left through the parking lot on US 1 at the stop sign. The post office and Wawa convenience store are located here.

US 1 was known as the Great Road in the 18th century. This was the easiest route for transporting people and supplies through the Brandywine Valley. General Knyphausen's troops marched along the Great Road and met Washington's men near here.

22.4 Turn right and cross US 1 at the light on the corner.

Across the street on US 1 and PA 100 is Hank's Restaurant, a nice lunch stop. The Brandywine River Hotel (610-388-1200) is here, as is the Brandywine River Museum (610-388-2700), open daily 9:30–4:30.

23.7 Right on Brintons Bridge Road. Go straight through the stop sign in Dilworthtown, where the last of the Battle of Brandywine was fought at nightfall.

The Dilworthtown Country Store, built in 1758 as a store and saddlery, is at this intersection. It is one of the oldest general stores in continuous operation in the country. Rumor has it that the counter, still in the store, was used as an operating table after the battle. The Dilworthtown Inn is next to the country store. It is reported that local people, loyal to the Continental Army, were briefly held captive here. The British wanted to prevent them from informing Washington that the British were not pursuing him.

Arden Forge, an 18th-century blacksmith shop, is also at this crossroads. The forge made arms during the French and Indian War as well as the American Revolution.

For a side trip, consider turning right here on Oakland Road. British and Hessian troops camped along this road after the battle. A short distance farther is the Brinton 1704 House (610-399-0913) at 1435 Oakland Road. This restored Quaker home, with medieval English architecture, is open to the public on summer weekends, 11–6. After your visit, return to the Dilworthtown crossroads and turn right on Brinton Bridge Road.

When you cross US 202 at 26.2 miles, the road becomes Dilworthtown Road.

29.1 **Right after crossing the railroad and creek onto Cheyney Road. This intersection is unmarked.**

29.9 **Right on Creek Road at Cheyney College and Tanguy Roads.**

32.0 **Left on Sweetwater Road.**

There is a pizza place and general store. Go straight on Cheyney College Road on the other side of the creek.

33.2 **Right at the T on Valley Road.**

33.9 **Left on Forge Road.**

35.0 **Straight across PA 352, New Middletown Road.**

35.4 **Straight on the bike path where the road turns right and becomes Painter Road.**

36.9 **End in the parking lot.**

IV
SCENIC BUCKS COUNTY

Scenic Bucks County

These three rides will take you along the Delaware River north of New Hope, Pennsylvania. You will also have the opportunity to visit Bucks County west of the Delaware, including Doylestown, the Mercer Museum, Peace Valley Park, and Tohickon Valley Park.

Chapter 10 heads north from New Hope along the Delaware Canal Towpath to Uhlerstown, Pennsylvania, where you will cross the river into Frenchtown, New Jersey. You will travel back to New Hope via the Delaware and Raritan Canal.

In chapter 11, "Ringing Rocks," you will see more of Bucks County. The ride begins in Tohickon State Park, adjacent to the Delaware River.

Chapter 12, "Arts and Crafts in Bucks County," begins in Peace Valley Park and travels on the outskirts of Doylestown, meandering to New Hope. On the return leg, you will go through Doylestown and have the chance to visit the Mercer Museum before heading back to Peace Valley.

Tours 10 and 12 both pass through New Hope and can be combined for a longer ride. The Towpath ride (10) and the Ringing Rocks ride (11) overlap on the Delaware Canal Towpath from Point Pleasant to Erwinna. I have mentioned overnight lodging at several points along the river, so it is easy to create a weekend ride by combining the routes. With more than 90 miles of paths and roads to use, you could put three or four days together if you wanted to spend at bit more time. It's a very pretty part of Pennsylvania, and there is much to see.

10
Delaware River Canal Towpath

Distance: *30 miles*
Difficulty: *Easy*
Terrain: *Mostly flat. Much of the route is unpaved, and this ride is best suited for mountain or hybrid bicycles.*
Location: *New Hope, Pennsylvania, 40 miles northeast of Philadelphia, 35 miles southeast of Allentown, 115 miles northeast of Harrisburg, and 100 miles southeast of Scranton.*
Of Special Interest: *The visitors center in New Hope (215-862-0758) can provide information on overnight lodgings and restaurants, as well as other information about the area.*

Mules that walked along the towpath pulled canal barges. At the visitors center, you can make arrangements to ride a mule-drawn boat on the river. A mule is the offspring of a female horse and a male donkey; the offspring of a female donkey and a male horse is a hinny. Both animals were used on the towpath, but mules were preferred, as they are stronger and more resistant to illness and injury than hinnies, horses, or donkeys. They are also extremely sure-footed, not particular about food, and can tolerate extreme temperatures.

Mules have a reputation for being stubborn, but those who work with them think this is due to bad handling. If a mule mistrusts or dislikes its trainer, it will not cooperate. However, once a bond is created, a mule is as loyal and obedient as any dog, according to one source.

Services: *New Hope has many restaurants and B&Bs. There are also restaurants in Point Pleasant and Frenchtown.*

There is camping in Tohickon Valley Park; see the Ringing Rocks ride for details.

The Lambertville House, a National Historic Inn, is located at 32 Bridge Street, P.O. Box 349, Lambertville, NJ 08530; 609-397-0200.

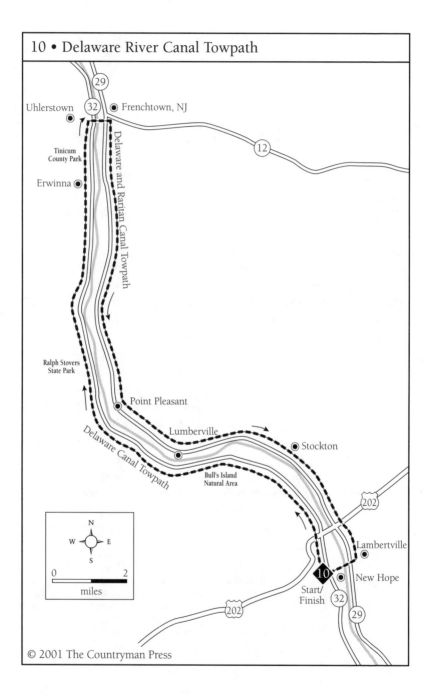

29

32 Uhlerstown ◉ ◉ Frenchtown, NJ

12

Delaware and Raritan Canal Towpath

Tinicum County Park

Erwinna ◉

Ralph Stovers State Park

Delaware Canal Towpath

◉ Point Pleasant

Lumberville

◉ Stockton

Bull's Island Natural Area

202

N
W · E
S

0   2
miles

202

Lambertville ◉

10
Start/ Finish

New Hope ◉

32

29

© 2001 The Countryman Press

Bicycle Shop: *New Hope Cyclery is at 186 Old York Road, New Hope, PA 18983; 215-862-6888.*

To Get There

From I-76, take exit 26, US 202, and go north. After about 33 miles, exit on PA 179 for New Hope. Turn left on PA 32. After about 1 mile, bear right on Towpath Road, where you can park.
From I-78, take exit 22 in Easton and follow signs for PA 611 South. Go south on PA 611 for about 12 miles and then turn south on PA 32. After about 16 miles, turn right on Cafferty Road in Point Pleasant. Turn left in about 1 mile into the parking lot for Tohickon Valley County Park.

In the 19th century, anthracite coal from central Pennsylvania was in great demand but barges could not navigate the Delaware and Schuylkill Rivers all the way to the mines. Modeled after canals in Europe and Asia, the Erie Canal opened in 1825 in New York. Its great success stimulated canal building in America, and construction began on a 1200-mile series of canals to connect Philadelphia, Pittsburgh, and Lake Erie. The Delaware Canal runs for 60 miles from Bristol, Pennsylvania, to Easton, Pennsylvania, where it connects with the Lehigh Canal. Barges could carry up to 70 tons of coal at a time as they were lowered or raised 165 feet through 23 locks.
A 30-mile trail extending from Frenchtown, New Jersey, to Washington Crossing, Pennsylvania, parallels the Delaware Canal on the east bank of the Delaware River. This was the feeder canal for New Jersey's 44-mile Raritan Canal, which delivered coal to New York City.
This ride starts in the middle of that stretch in New Hope, Pennsylvania, and travels north to Frenchtown, New Jersey. There, you will cross the river into Pennsylvania, turn south, and ride back to New Hope.

The Ride

0.0 Start in New Hope, Pennsylvania, on Towpath Street on PA 32. Go north on the towpath.
Immigrant laborers, mostly Irish, dug canals in America by hand. Most of the canals were 50 to 75 feet wide and 6 or 7 feet deep.

The flat towpath along the canal makes a great ride for a beginning cyclist.

In the 1840s and 1850s, over 3,000 mule-drawn barges and over 1 million tons of coal were transported along the Delaware River every year.

7.4 Cross Point Pleasant Pike.

There are shops and restaurants in Point Pleasant.

10.6 Pass through Smithtown where you will find locks 15 and 16.

The canals operated via a series of locks. Water was pumped into or out of a lock to raise or lower boats to the level of the next lock. Then the adjoining gates were opened and mules pulled barges from one lock to the next.

12.2 Pass through Erwinna.

Many of the towns along the Delaware River pre-date the canal. Some date back to the early 18th century.

You will pass the Golden Pheasant Inn here, with an expensive full-service restaurant.

12.7 Tinicum County Park is on the right.

There are picnic tables, water, and toilets.

14.6 Right on Uhlerstown Hill Road.

Uhlerstown Covered Bridge is the only covered bridge that crosses the Delaware Canal.

14.9 Left on PA 32 at the T.

14.9 Immediately turn right on Bridge Street and cross the Delaware River into Frenchtown, New Jersey.

15.2 Right on the Delaware and Raritan Canal Towpath.

By the mid-1800s, steam engines began to replace mules. Canal transportation reached a peak in the last quarter of the 19th century and was eventually replaced by trains. Canals continued to operate until the 1930s. At that point, the state governments took over and rehabilitated the canal for water supply. The Delaware Canal State Park was created in 1940, and the Delaware Raritan Canal State Park was created in 1974.

29.7 Enter the parking lot of the Lambertville Station Restaurant and leave the towpath. Right on Bridge Street in Lambertville, New Jersey, and cross the river into New Hope, Pennsylvania.

29.8 Right on PA 32.

30.7 End on Towpath Street.

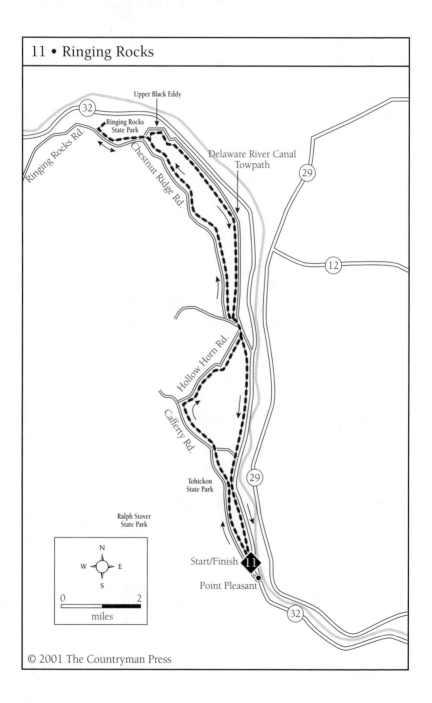

Upper Black Eddy

Ringing Rocks
State Park

Delaware River Canal
Towpath

Ringing Rocks Rd.

Chestnut Ridge Rd.

Hollow Horn Rd.

Cafferty Rd.

Tohickon
State Park

Ralph Stover
State Park

N
W — E
S

0   2
miles

Start/Finish 11

Point Pleasant

© 2001 The Countryman Press

11
Ringing Rocks

Distance: 26 miles
Difficulty: Easy to Moderate
Terrain: Mostly flat with two hills. After going through the Erwinna Covered Bridge at 5.7 miles, you will climb 400 feet to Red Cliff Road at 8.3 miles. The second hill is the 250-foot climb up Cafferty Road from 25 to 26 miles. The Delaware Canal Towpath is unpaved and is best suited for a mountain or hybrid bicycle.
Location: Tohickon Valley County Park, Point Pleasant, Pennsylvania. 40 miles northeast of Philadelphia, 35 miles east of Allentown, 120 miles northeast of Harrisburg, and 100 miles south of Scranton.
Of Special Interest: Ringing Rocks Park is essentially a sea of boulders. The main attraction is a field where you will find small groups of people gleefully smacking the boulders with hammers. The sound from some of the rocks is the dull thud you would expect. But many of the boulders resonate when hit and ring like bells.

This boulder field began as a lake. The sediment at the bottom eventually solidified into shale. Later, magma from volcanoes hardened the shale. During the Ice Age, repeated freeze-thaw cycles broke up the shale into large boulders and frost heaves pushed them to the surface. The cold temperatures and rushing meltwater may have prevented the accumulation of soil and plant growth.

Water penetrated a couple of inches into the rocks and reacted chemically with some of the elements to form a kind of clay. This clay takes up more space than the unchanged rock. So the top 2 inches or so of rock expanded and formed a tight skin that is under more stress than the internal rock. This, plus the high content of iron, causes the ringing.

Boulders that are in the sun most of the time usually ring better than those in the shade because the water is not retained as long. So climb out to the middle of the field with your hammer and give it a try.

Don't worry about not having a hammer with you when you visit Ringing Rocks. You will find one lying around or there will be someone who is willing to share theirs with you. You can tell the best rocks by the scuff marks from previous rock ringers.

Services: Tohickon Valley Park has campsites and cabins available for a fee. Picnic tables, water, and toilets are also available.

Colonial Woods Family Camping is in Upper Black Eddy at 345 Lonely Cottage Drive, Upper Black Eddy, PA 18972; 610-847-5808. It received Woodalls Campground Directory's 5-star rating. Also in Upper Black Eddy is Ringing Rocks Family Campground (610-982-5552).

Tattersall Inn in Point Pleasant is located at 16 Cafferty Road, P.O. Box 569, Point Pleasant, PA 18950; 215-297-8233.

There are numerous places for overnight lodging in New Hope and Doylestown.

Where you turn onto the towpath, there is a general store and deli in Upper Black Eddy. It makes a great place for a lunch stop. There are also services in Point Pleasant, including places to get food and beverages.

Bicycle Shop: The closest bicycle shop is in New Hope, PA. New Hope Cyclery is located at 186 Old York Road, New Hope, PA 18938; 215-862-6888.

To Get There

From I-76, take exit 26, US 202 North. After about 33 miles, exit on PA 179 for New Hope. Turn left on PA 32. Follow PA 32 North about 8 miles. Turn left on Cafferty Road in Point Pleasant. In about 1 mile, turn left into the parking lot for Tohickon Valley County Park.

From I-78, take exit 22 in Easton, Pennsylvania, and follow signs for PA 611 South. Go south on PA 611 for about 12 miles and then turn onto PA 32 South. After about 16 miles, turn right on Cafferty Road in Point Pleasant. Turn left in about 1 mile into the parking lot for Tohickon Valley County Park.

You will see more of Bucks County on this ride. The starting point is Tohickon State Park. The route heads north from the park through two covered bridges and the rural, mostly wooded, rolling hills of Bucks County. A brief side trip takes you to Ringing Rocks State Park. You will head into Upper Black Eddy, where you will turn south and follow the Delaware Canal Towpath back to Tohickon State Park.

Tohickon Park abuts High Rocks and Ralph Stover State Parks. High Rocks was added to the state parks system through the donation of Doylestown native James Michener. Its 200-foot-tall cliffs are popular with technical rock climbers. Ralph Stover owned and operated a water-powered mill in this area in the 18th century. Parts of the mill remain within the park. You can tour the Erwin-Stover House, built in 1800, by appointment; 215-489-5133.

The Ride

0.0 **Start at the parking lot of Tohickon State Park on Cafferty Road. Tory Road crosses Cafferty Road at 0.8 mile.**

Continue straight unless you would like to take a detour to High Rocks and Ralph Stover State Parks. Then you can turn left on Tory Road. In 2 miles, you will be in High Rocks. At the T, turn left on Stover Park Road and you will enter Ralph Stover Park after crossing a covered bridge.

Back on the route, you will cross Smithtown Road at 1.5 miles.

2.0 **Left to stay on Cafferty Road where Twin Lear Road enters from the right. Cross Dark Hollow Road at 2.4 miles.**

3.1 **Right where Hollow Horn Road joins from the left.**

Go through Frankenfield Covered Bridge. Built in 1872 across Tinicum Creek, it is one of the longest covered bridges in Bucks County.

3.3 **Right on Hollow Horn Road.**

4.6 **Right on Headquarters Road.**

4.7 **Left to stay on Headquarters Road.**

5.5 **Left on Geigel Hill Road at the T.**

Go through the Erwinna Covered Bridge at 5.7 miles. The listing

The Erwinna Covered Bridge is the shortest one in Bucks County.

in the National Historic Register for this bridge gives the construction date as 1871, but county records show evidence that it was built in 1832. It crosses Lodi Creek and is the shortest covered bridge in Bucks County.

6.0 *Right on Upper Tinicum Church Road. Bear right to stay on Tinicum Church Road at Roaring Rocks Road at 6.9 miles.*

7.6 *Bear right again at Perry Auger Road.*

7.7 *Then bear left at Uhlerstown Hill Road and cross Swamp Creek, still on Tinicum Church Road.*
Tinicum Lutheran Church is on the right at 7.8 miles.

8.3 *Left on Red Cliff Road.*

8.4 *Right to get back on Upper Tinicum Church Road at Union School Road.*

9.1 *Straight to cross Lodi Hill Road. Upper Tinicum Church Road becomes Chestnut Ridge Road here.*

10.8 *Left on Bridgeton Hill Road at the T to visit Ringing Rocks Park.*
If you wish to go straight to the towpath, turn right instead and go downhill into the town of Upper Black Eddy.

11.3 *Right on Ringing Rocks Road.*

11.9 *Right into the parking area for Ringing Rocks Park.*

You can lock your bike up at the end of the parking area, or you can ride or walk along the path leading to the boulder field. The path is a dirt trail and quite rough.

In 1890, Dr J. J. Ott located rocks that rang with the pitches of an octave scale. Accompanied by a brass band, he tapped out tunes with a hammer for the members of the Buckwampum Historical Society. This marked the beginning of rock music.

12.4 *Left out of the parking area back out onto Ringing Rocks Road.*

13.0 *Left on Bridgeton Hill Road. Pass Chestnut Ridge Road at 13.6 miles.*

14.3 *Follow the road to the left into the town of Upper Black Eddy. Cross the canal at 14.5 miles.*

Immediately after the canal there is a grocery store and deli on the right. The towpath is between the canal and the store. Really! That little footpath is it.

15.9 *Red Cliff Road crosses the canal here.*

On the other side of the canal you will find the Dogwood Haven Campground. A second bridge crosses the canal at Jugtown Hill Road at 16.9 miles. Uhlerstown Covered Bridge is at 17.8 miles at Uhlerstown Hill Road. This bridge was built in 1832 and it is the only covered bridge that crosses the Delaware Canal. It has windows on both sides.

18.7 *Tinicum County Park is on the right.*

There are picnic tables, water, and toilets. You can also visit the Erwin-Stover House. There is another bridge across the canal at 19.6 miles in the town of Erwinna. PA 32 crosses the canal path at 20.3 miles.

25.0 *Leave the canal path and cross the Delaware River on Point Pleasant Pike.*

25.1 *Right on PA 32.*

25.2 *Bear left off of PA 32 on Cafferty Road and climb up the hill.*

26.3 *Left into the parking area of Tohickon State Park.*

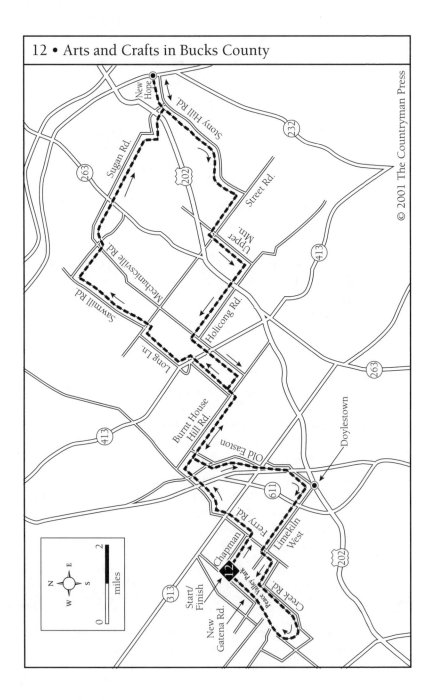

© 2001 The Countryman Press

Arts and Crafts in Bucks County

Distance: 40 miles

Difficulty: Moderate

Terrain: Moderately rolling throughout. All roads are paved. Suitable for any bicycle.

Location: Peace Valley Park, 3 miles northwest of Doylestown and 30 miles north of Philadelphia, 35 miles south of Allentown, 115 miles east of Harrisburg and 100 miles south of Scranton.

Of Special Interest: The solar-heated Peace Valley Nature Center (170 Chapman Road, Doylestown, PA 18909; 215-345-7860) is open Tuesday through Saturday, 9–5. There is a store and some very nice exhibits about the area. The 9 miles of footpaths are not open to bicycles. Trail maps are available in the nature center. You can also visit the gardens around the nature center, including a pond and a duck blind.

Much of Lake Galena's shoreline is a wildlife refuge, and it is possible to see over 250 species of birds along the trails. This is considered to be an excellent place to learn bird-watching.

The Mercer Museum and the Moravian Pottery and Tile Works are nearby in Doylestown. Moravian Pottery and Tile Works is a working history museum. Henry C. Mercer, who built the tile works, was a major influence on the Arts and Crafts movement in late 19th-century America.

Victorian eclecticism was popular in the last half of the 1900s. Decoration was ornate, detailed, and quite dark. Also, the industrial revolution had introduced machine-made objects from art to furniture. Mercer and others sought to return to simpler lines and encouraged slight "flaws" in decor that would make objects look handmade. Today, the tile works still uses Mercer's techniques to produce wonderful tiles and mosaics.

The carriage house of Fonthill Mansion is now a gift shop and tourist information center.

Moravian Pottery and Tile works is located at 130 Swamp Road, PA 313, Doylestown; 215-345-6722. It is about 0.5 mile east of PA 611. The Mercer Museum is right next door at 84 South Pine Street; 215-345-0210.

Fonthill Castle, also adjacent to the tile works, was Mercer's home. It houses thousands of art objects that Mercer collected during his life. Both Fonthill and the Mercer Museum were constructed out of hand-mixed concrete. All three Mercer buildings are open to the public for a fee Monday through Saturday, 10–4, except holidays. The grounds of Fonthill are open to the public from sunrise to dusk. There are picnic tables and walking trails available at no charge.

Services: *Peace Valley Park has picnic benches, water, and toilets. You will arrive in New Hope in about 16 miles. There are many choices for food and beverages on Main Street. There are also many services in Doylestown, including a mini-mart at 31 miles.*

Bicycle Shop: *New Hope Cyclery is located at 186 Old York Road, New Hope; 215-862-6888.*

To Get There

Take PA 611 North. From Philadelphia, follow Broad Street until it becomes PA 611. From I-76, take the Willow Grove exit for PA 611 and go north about 12 miles. From US 202, follow PA 611 about 1.5 mile.

From the north, take I-78 to Easton and go south on PA 611.

Exit from PA 611 on PA 313, Swamp Road. At the top of the ramp, turn left to go west toward Dublin. In 2 miles, turn left on New Galena Road, following signs to Peace Valley Park. Turn left on Chapman Road in 0.7 mile, following signs to the Nature Center. At the bottom of the hill in 0.3 mile, turn left into the nature center parking lot just past the stop sign.

Peace Valley Park surrounds Lake Galena, about 3 miles northwest of Doylestown and 25 miles north of Philadelphia. There are 9 miles of footpaths and a 5-mile hike-and-bike trail.

The Ride

0.0 *Start in the parking area for Peace Valley Nature Center. Turn left on Chapman Road out of the parking area.*

0.1 *Cross the pedestrian bridge over Lake Galena.*

0.8 *Left on Ferry Road. Go straight across Swamp Road, PA 313, at the traffic light.*

Follow Ferry Road as it turns left and then right. You will pass under PA 611. At this point the name of the road changes to Point Pleasant Pike. This is a pretty, residential area.

3.3 *Right on Burnt House Hill Road immediately after passing Gayman School.*

4.3 *Bear right to join Landisville Road at the stop sign.*

4.4 *Straight to stay on Burnt House Hill Road where Landisville Road turns right.*

Note that Superman's girlfriend lives on Lois Lane on the right at 4.7 miles.

4.8 *Go straight across Cold Spring Creamery Road.*

5.5 Left on Hansell Road just after the top of the hill.

6.7 Left just before PA 413 on West Long Lane. Turn into the new housing development and follow the road as it twists and turns.

7.1 Straight across PA 413, Durham Road to stay on Long Lane.

8.4 Right on Street Road at the stop sign.

8.6 Cross Paunnacussing Creek, then turn left immediately onto Sawmill Road.

This is a pleasant, narrow road with no traffic.

10.8 Right on Sugan Road. Go straight across Greenhill Road at the stop sign.

You will pass horse farms to the left.

11.8 Left to stay on Sugan Road at Mechanicsville Road at the stop sign.

11.9 Right to stay on Sugan, following the arrows to stay on the main road.

13.0 Go straight across PA 263, Upper York Road, and then jog a bit to the left. Bear right immediately after crossing PA 263 at the Y to stay on Sugan Road. Phillips Mill Road is to the left.

14.9 Right to stay on Sugan where Kitchen Lane joins from the left.

15.1 Left to stay on Sugan Road. Kitchen Lane continues straight and Wilshire Road is to the right.

15.5 Straight across US 202, Lower York Road.

15.7 Straight across PA 179, West Bridge Road.

15.8 Bear left just before the railroad tracks on Mechanic Street, James Magill Way. Then cross Aquetong Creek.

15.9 Bear left on Mechanic Street at the Y.

16.5 Take the next left on Stockton Avenue. Cross the Aquetong Creek.

16.6 Right on Ferry Street.

This is New Hope. William Penn deeded the land to Richard Heath in 1710. Cross the Delaware Canal.

16.7 *Right on Main Street.*

This is the main shopping area. You will find many places to get food and drinks.

16.8 *Right on Mechanic Street, James Magill Way. Cross the canal. Go straight where New Street joins from the left at 16.9 miles. Cross Stockton Avenue.*

17.5 *Bear left at Stony Hill Road and go up the hill.*

Do not cross the creek or the railroad tracks.

19.4 *Cross Aquetong Road.*

20.6 *Right on Street Road. Go straight across the railroad tracks at 21.2 miles.*

21.8 *Left on Upper Mountain Road.*

There are horse farms on both sides of the road here.

23.0 *Right at the T on Holicong Road. Cross US 202 at 23.7 miles.*

25.2 *Left on Mechanicsville Road. Go straight across PA 413, Durham Road.*

26.6 *Right on Burnt House Hill Road. Cross Cold Spring Creamery Road at 27.9 miles.*

28.9 *Left on Dillon Road.*

29.5 *Left on Old Easton Road.*

29.8 *Bear right to stay on Old Easton Road.*

30.2 *Bear right to stay on Old Easton Road. Cross Swamp Road, PA 313, at 30.8 miles.*

Turn left here to visit the Moravian Pottery and Tile Works.

30.9 *Left on Chapman Avenue.*

31.2 *Right on North Street. Cross East Road, Old Dublin Pike.*

31.8 *Bear right on Lacey Avenue. Then go straight on Main Street, Old SR 611. The name changes to Union Street. Cross Broad Street.*

32.5 *Right on West Street. Go straight across PA 611.*

The name of the road changes to Limekiln Road.

34.4 *Left on Ferry Road.*

34.9 *Right on Limekiln Pike.*

35.6 *Left on Creek Road.*

You will pass a marina on the right at 36.4 miles where there is a snack concession, water, and toilets. Get on the hike-and-bike trail at the end of the parking lot and continue around the lake.

37.0 *Cross the dam on the hike-and-bike trail.*

37.4 *Follow the hike-and-bike trail to the right.*

38.5 *Straight onto New Galena Road.*

39.6 *Right on Chapman Road.*

39.9 *Left into the parking lot at the nature center.*

The Poconos

The Poconos region of the rolling Appalachian foothills is the most popular vacation destination in Pennsylvania. Hunting and fishing are very popular, as are rafting and canoeing. There are hundreds of miles of hiking and mountain-biking trails. The resorts are popular in the summer and during ski season. It's also a great place for general rest and relaxation.

State forest covers much of the area, helping to keep the area green and lush. On these two rides, you will see rolling, wooded roads that show much of the best of the Poconos.

A word of warning, however: I do not recommend riding these routes in July and August, the height of the tourist season. There are only a few through roads, and these are narrow and rolling with many twisting turns. Off-season, they are charming, but they are not large enough to handle the traffic that pours into the area in the heat of midsummer. The mountain laurel and rhododendrons are in bloom in late May and early June, and the leaves are lovely in late autumn. Those are the best times to enjoy these rides.

The rides overlap on PA 402. At 26.4 miles on the Promised Land ride, you will cross the Pocono climb at 9.8 miles. Combining the two routes results in a loop of about 86 miles. You can create a 2- or 3-day trip with overnight stays in Promised Land, Canadensis, Dingman's Ferry, Otter Lake, or Lake Wallenpaupack.

13

Promised Land State Park

Distance: 55 miles

Difficulty: Moderate

Terrain: Moderately rolling throughout. All roads are paved. Suitable for any bicycle.

Location: Promised Land State Park, 20 miles southeast of Scranton, 100 miles north of Philadelphia, 50 miles north of Allentown, 130 miles northwest of Harrisburg.

Of Special Interest: Promised Land State Park has many miles of trails. You can get a park map at the park office. Mountain biking is allowed on many of the trails. There is also a swimming beach open during daylight hours in the summer.

There are many places offering guided horseback riding. The one closest to this ride is in Mount Pocono, 10 miles south of Canadensis, mile 10. Carson's Riding Stable is on PA 611; 570-595-0604.

You can also go rafting or canoeing on the Delaware River. Adventure Sports (1-800-487-2628) is in Milford, about 20 miles east of Promised Land State Park.

Services: Promised Land State Park has camping and cabins. Also, there are picnic benches, drinking water, toilets, and a food concession stand.

The village of Promised Land has several motels, B&Bs, cottages, restaurants, and a couple of general stores. Hall's Inn (570-675-3429) on PA 390 is one of the nicest places. They also have a restaurant.

Otter Lake Campground is about 1 mile off the route at 17.8 miles. Instead of turning left to stay on Snow Hill Road, go straight on Marshall Creek Road for 1 mile.

On the ride, you will find options for food in the town of Canadensis at 10 miles.

Pickerel Inn and General Store is on the right at 27.8 miles. They

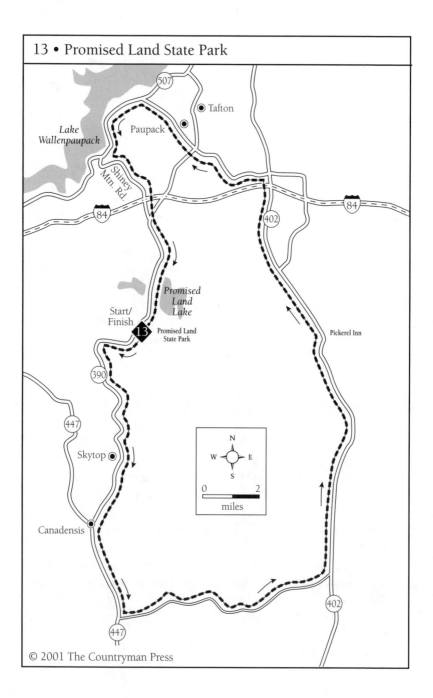

13 • Promised Land State Park

Lake
Wallenpaupack

507

Tafton

Paupack

Shiney
Mtn. Rd.

84

84

402

Promised
Land
Lake

Start/
Finish

13 Promised Land
State Park

Pickerel Inn

390

447

Skytop

N
W E
S

0   2
miles

Canadensis

447

402

© 2001 The Countryman Press

have a small deli, and they rent rooms above the store. There are also a couple of small restaurants at mile 31 and again at mile 39.
Bicycle Shops: *Cedar Bicycle is about 25 miles east on I-84 at 629 Pittston Ave, Scranton, PA 18505-4102; 570-344-3416. Action Outfitters on US 6 and PA 209 in Milford is 22 miles west on I-84; 570-296-6657. Pocono Bikes, on PA 940 in Pocono Lake is about 10 miles southwest of Canadensis; 570-646-9443.*

To Get There

From I-84, take exit 7, PA 390 South. The park office is on the right at the intersection of PA 390 and Lower Lake Road in 5 miles.

You can get on I-84 in Scranton from I-476 and I-81.

The first European inhabitants of this area were a group of Shakers, a religious sect who came here from New England. The Shakers cleared the land of trees only to find it too rocky to farm. When the colony failed, they bitterly named the area "The Promised Land."

Timber barons came next and clear-cut thousands of acres. This resulted in severe erosion and rampant forest fires. Much of the native wildlife migrated or died. The Commonwealth of Pennsylvania purchased the land in 1902 with the intention of protecting the plants and wildlife that remained and reclaiming the rest. The first park facilities were open to the public in 1905.

In the 1930s, Franklin Roosevelt founded the Civilian Conservation Corps, (CCC). This nonmilitary service employed young men to build railroads, bridges, and facilities on public lands as well as maintain wilderness areas. The CCC built most of the current park buildings and planted thousands of trees.

You will ride in and out of the Delaware State Forest on this ride, along the roads first built by loggers and then used by the CCC. Fortunately, today they are deeply wooded.

Along the way, you will see much of the tourist industry that has grown here along with the young trees. Many hidden, gated summer communities lurk in the woods next to the road. You will also see motels, restaurants, and other tourist amenities. Some of these are opulent, and some have seen much better days. Still others have never had "better" days. However, there are also many quaint, homey places that are very inviting.

The Ride

0.0 **Start at the park office for Promised Land State Park on PA 390 and Pickerel Point Road/Lower Lake Road. Go south on PA 390.**

At 6.5 miles, the road crosses a small creek leading into Mountain Lake. This is part of Sky Top Lodge. There is a walking path around the lake, and there are benches next to the road.

You'll soar down the road into Canadensis at around 9.5 miles.

9.8 **Left on PA 447 in Canadensis. There are several choices for a food stop here.**

PA 447 parallels Brodhead Creek, and there are some nice views to your right.

13.0 **Left on Snow Hill Road.**

The signpost for Snow Hill Road is on the left side of the road. On the right is Clark Road, which is unpaved. There is also a sign for Otter Creek Campground, located at the top of Snow Hill Road.

Climb steeply up the hill. The summit is around 16 miles. This is also where you will reenter Delaware State Forest. This is a lovely, quiet road with very little traffic. There are no houses in the state forest.

18.0 **Left to stay on Snow Hill Road although there is no signpost.**

Leave the main road here, now named Marshalls Creek Road. Right is Hiawatha Lane, which is unpaved.

There are a couple of mailboxes on the left. There is also a huge rock painted yellow bearing the name "Camp William Penn."

Otter Lake Campground is straight ahead on Marshalls Creek Road in about a mile.

20.0 **Cross Big Bushkill Creek.**

You will also cross trailheads along this road in Pennel Run State Nature Area.

Lake Wallenpaupack is a popular site for boating, fishing, and general vacationing.

22.3 Left on PA 402 at the T and stop sign.

There is a signpost here confirming that you were on Snow Hill Road.

PA 402 can be busy at times. As you ride farther north, traffic will dwindle, and the trees become larger, with many more conifers.

To your right at 26.4 is a parking lot. There is a public toilet here. Just after the parking lot is Old Bushkill Road, mile 11.8 on the Pocono Mountain climb.

Pass Porter Lake Hunting and Fishing Club on your right. You would have a lovely view of the lake if your vision were not obstructed by the barbed wire–topped chain-link fence. Are we being kept out or are wild animals being kept in? Perhaps it's really Jurassic Park. Keep your eyes peeled for velociraptors.

On the right at 27.7 miles is Silver Lake/Edgemere Road, mile 10.4 on the Pocono Mountain climb.

Just past Edgemere Road you will come upon Pickerel Inn and General Store, a small deli. There are also a couple of places to eat at 31 miles.

37.0 *Cross under I-84 at 37 miles.*

37.9 *Next left on SR 4004, Blooming Grove Road.*

42.8 *Straight across PA 390 where the road name changes to Gumbletown Road. You are finally heading downhill.*

45.4 *Left on PA 507.*

48.9 *Left on Shiney Mountain Road.*

There is a huge sign here for Saint Veronica Roman Catholic Church and a small sign for the airport. This is another steep uphill climb.

51.7 *Straight across I-84.*

52.5 *Right on PA 390. Pass through the village of Promised Land.*

56.2 *End at the park office on Lower Lake Road.*

14
Pocono Mountain Ramble

Distance: *32 miles*
Difficulty: *Moderate*
Terrain: *Rolling to hilly. All roads are paved. Suitable for any bicycle.*
Location: *George W. Childs Recreation Area parking area, 2 miles northwest of Dingmans Ferry on Silver Lake Road, State Route 2004 (SR 2004). About 75 miles east of Scranton, 100 miles north of Philadelphia, 65 miles north of Allentown, 150 miles northeast of Harrisburg.*
Of Special Interest: *This is a pleasant rolling ramble through the woods above the Delaware River. Bushkill Falls is a commercial operation. There are several hikes through the hills, but there is an admission charge.*
Services: *Pickerel Inn and General Store is less than 0.1 mile off the route, to the right on PA 402 at 9.8 miles. Bushkill Falls has more than one option for food, about 0.1 mile to the right at 21.2 miles.*

The town of Dingmans Ferry is about 3 miles from the start of the ride, to the right downhill from George W. Child Recreation Area. There are many places to eat or spend the night.
Bicycle Shop: *The closest bike shop is Action Outfitters on US 6 and PA 209 in Milford; 570-296-6657. Go into Dingmans Ferry and take US 209 North for 5 miles.*

To Get There

From I-84, take exit 6, US 6 South for 2 miles to Milford. Take US 209 South for 5 miles to Dingmans Ferry.

From I-80, take exit 52, Marshall's Creek, on US 209 North 20 miles to Dingmans Ferry.

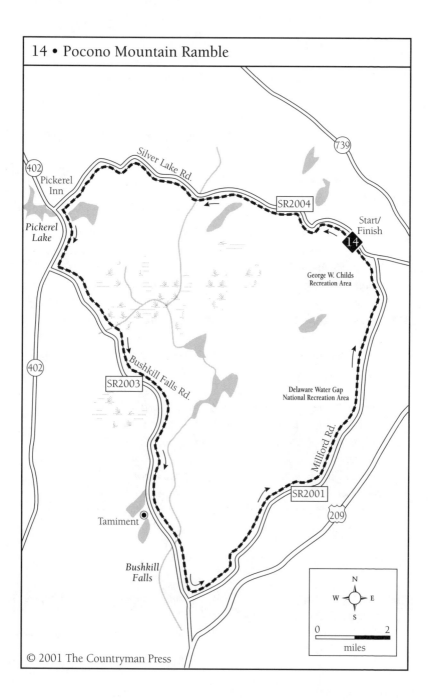

739

402
Pickerel
Inn

Silver Lake Rd.

SR2004

*Pickerel
Lake*

Start/
Finish

14

402

George W. Childs
Recreation Area

Bushkill Falls Rd.

SR2003

Delaware Water Gap
National Recreation Area

Millford Rd.

Tamiment

SR2001

209

*Bushkill
Falls*

N
W E
S

0   2
miles

In Dingmans Ferry, go west 1 mile on PA 739. Turn left on Silver Lake Road, SR 4001. After about 1 mile you will see parking areas on the left for George W. Child Recreation Area. Park in one of these.

The Delaware River runs through a deep gorge from Port Jervis, New York, to Delaware Water Gap National Recreation Area. I have started this ride above the steepest part of the ascent from the river at Dingmans Ferry, at George W. Child Recreation Area. Whether you work your thigh muscles or drive, you should go all the way down to Dingmans Ferry and see some of the great scenery along the Delaware River. There are also numerous scenic views of waterfalls along the way.

The Ride

0.0 *Start by turning left from the parking area and heading northwest, away from Dingmans Ferry, on Silver Lake Road, SR 2004.*

That's Nyce Lake on the right at 0.8 mile. At 3.2 miles, you will cross Dingmans Creek, a feeder of Silver Lake, on the left.

9.8 *Left on PA 402.*

There is a Sunoco Station and Pickerel Inn to the right on PA 402. It's about 0.1 mile away. You can get food and drinks.

You will pass Porter Lake Hunting and Fishing Club on PA 402 at 10.1 miles. There would be a nice view of Porter Lake if you didn't have to look at it through the barbed wire and chain-link fence.

11.2 *Left on Bushkill Falls Road, SR 2003.*

Tamiment Resort is on the right at 18.8 miles. The entrance to Bushkill Falls is on the right at 21.2 miles. There is a restaurant and a snack store.

21.5 *Left on Milford Road, SR 2001.*

22.8 *Left to stay on Milford Road where Brodread joins from the right.*

This road twists and rolls through the woods. There are private communities scattered throughout the area, but they are set well back from the road.

Silver Lake Road connects Dingman's Ferry to the wooded plateau above and west of the Delaware River.

32.3 Left at the T and stop sign on Silver Lake Road, SR 2004.

32.9 Left into the parking area for George W. Child Recreation Area.

VI

THE ENDLESS MOUNTAINS

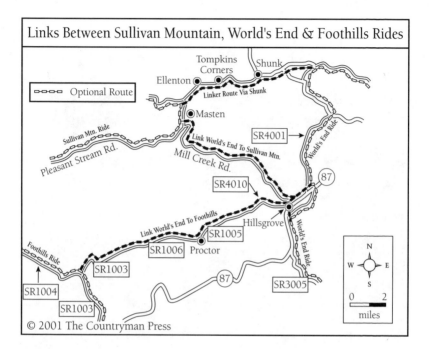

Links Between Sullivan Mountain, World's End & Foothills Rides

The Endless Mountains

The wooded rolling highlands of north central Pennsylvania are called the Endless Mountains. The region covers most of the area between the Susquehenny and Allegheny Rivers, and much of it is state forest, purchased in the 1930s from the Central Pennsylvania Lumber Company. A great attraction is the extensive, well-maintained roads that cross the forests, allowing easy access to the deep woods.

The following five rides are through the eastern part of the Endless Mountains.

Three of these routes—chapters 15, 16, and 17—can be linked easily if you want to spend several days exploring the area. (See page 146 for directions.) There are many campgrounds and plenty of hotels, guesthouses and B&Bs throughout the area.

15
The Rolling Foothills

Distance: *33 miles*
Difficulty: *Moderate to Difficult*
Terrain: *Rolling to hilly. You begin this ride by climbing 500 feet in 3 miles. A climb of 300 feet in 2 miles follows a 1.5-mile downhill rest. The next hill is up Sugar Camp Road, a climb of 500 feet from 8.5 to 10.5 miles. After that, the route is rolling and more downhill than up, until the climb of 350 feet to the top of Grammers Road from 29.1 to 30.6 miles. All roads on this route are paved and are suitable for any bicycle.*
Location: *Faxon is in the eastern part of greater Williamsport, 175 miles northwest of Philadelphia, 120 miles northwest of Allentown, 90 miles north of Harrisburg, and 90 miles west of Scranton.*
Services: *You will find a number of hotels, food stores, and restaurants in Williamsport. Along the route, there are public toilets at Rose Valley Lake. The Warrensville Country Store sells snacks and sandwiches at 26.8 miles.*
Bicycle Shop: *The Williamsport Bicycle Center is at 909 Main Street; 570-323-1153.*

To Get There

From I-80, exit 31, Milton, go north on I-180 about 30 miles. Take the Faxon exit, continuing straight on Northway Drive, State Road 2029 (SR 2029). After crossing Four Mile Drive, SR 2018, go 0.35 mile and park at the municipal park on the left.

This route begins in the town of Faxon, part of greater Williamsport. First, you will ride through rural residential areas. The houses become

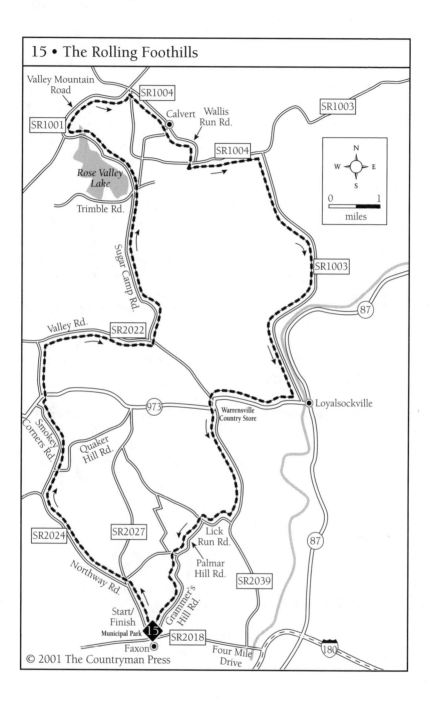

Valley Mountain Road

SR1004

SR1001

Calvert

Wallis Run Rd.

SR1003

SR1004

N
W ✦ E
S

0   1
miles

Rose Valley Lake

Trimble Rd.

Sugar Camp Rd.

SR1003

87

Valley Rd.

SR2022

973

Warrensville Country Store

Loyalsockville

Smokey Corners Rd.

Quaker Hill Rd.

SR2024

SR2027

Lick Run Rd.

Palmar Hill Rd.

SR2039

87

Northway Rd.

Grammer's Hill Rd.

Start/ Finish

Municipal Park

15

SR2018

Faxon

Four Mile Drive

180

© 2001 The Countryman Press

fewer in number as the farm fields become larger. When you turn onto Sugar Camp Road at 8 miles, the area is wooded and undeveloped. By 12 miles, you will ride along the shore of Rose Valley Lake, a popular recreation area in the summer. Here you will change direction, pass affluent housing developments, and enjoy a lovely flat ride along Loyalsock Creek. Finally you will ride up to a plateau just before you return to Faxon.

The Ride

0.0 *Start by turning left from the parking lot on Northway Drive, State Road (SR) 2029.*

0.7 *Left at Northway Road and Northway Road.*

This is not a typo. You will see the street sign on the left side of the road. Leave SR 2029, turning onto SR 2024.

3.2 *Right at Smokey Corner Road, Township 488 (T 488).*

3.6 *Bear left to stay on Smokey Corner Road.*

The main road turns right and becomes Quaker Hill Road.

5.0 *Right on PA 973 at the T.*

5.2 *Left on Klump Road. Here you are in rolling farmland.*

6.2 *Right at the T on Valley Road, SR 2022. This road is unmarked.*

8.0 *Make a hard backward left onto Sugar Camp Road where Valley Road begins a hard turn to the right. Cross the bridge and continue straight, next to Sugar Camp Run.*

This small road takes you into undeveloped woods. It also takes you uphill. The summit is in about 2 miles. On your way down to Rose Valley Lake there are some nice views to the left.

11.3 *An unmarked road (Trimble Road) joins from the left. Both roads immediately bend to the right. In less than 0.1 mile, bear left to stay on Sugar Camp Road where Trimble Road continues straight.*

Rose Valley Lake's east access point is on the left at 11.7 miles. There are parking and public toilets.

Follow the road as it crosses Rose Valley Lake on a cement

The view from the summit of Sugar Camp Road

causeway at 13.0 miles. There are lovely views on both sides as you cross the causeway. This is particularly beautiful in the fall.

13.7 Right at the T on Valley Mountain Road, SR 1001.

You are entering an affluent Williamsport suburb with many large, new homes.

15.5 Right on SR 1004.

15.6 Left to stay on SR 1004 at Cemetery Road.

The area becomes more rural as you follow SR 1004. The name of the road becomes Wallis Run Road at 16.6 miles. This is pretty, rolling farmland.

16.7 Bear left to stay on SR 1004.

19.2 Right on SR 1003 to Loyalsockville.

Straight ahead, SR 1003 goes east to Hillsgrove. This is a linker route to the World's End ride. See the end of this section.

SR 1003 to Loyalsockville is a pretty, flat ride for the next 5 miles. Loyalsock Creek is visible to your left most of the way.

24.9 Right at the stop sign on PA 973 West.

A left turn would take you over Loyalsock Creek to PA 87. The town of Loyalsockville is to the right, south on PA 87.

26.7 Left at the T to stay on PA 973 West in Warrensville.

Warrensville Country Store is on the left at 26.8 miles. Enter through the rear of the building for snacks and sandwiches.

26.9 Continue straight on SR 2039 where PA 973 turns right.

29.4 Right on Lick Run Road, SR 2031, and cross Lick Run.

This is a pretty, rural area.

29.5 Left after crossing the creek to stay on SR 2031.

29.9 Bear left and go uphill on Palmer Hill Road.

30.9 Left at the T on Grammers Road.

Enjoy the panoramic view of the farms in the area and Williamsport in the distance. The road is flat for a mile, and then you will enjoy a pleasant downhill run into Faxon.

32.5 Right at the T on Four Mile Drive, SR 2018.

There is traffic on this road, but there is a shoulder and you won't be here very long.

32.7 Right at the traffic light on Northway Drive.

33.0 Left into the parking lot of the municipal park.

Linking Routes

For directions on linking this ride with chapters 16 and 17, see page 146.

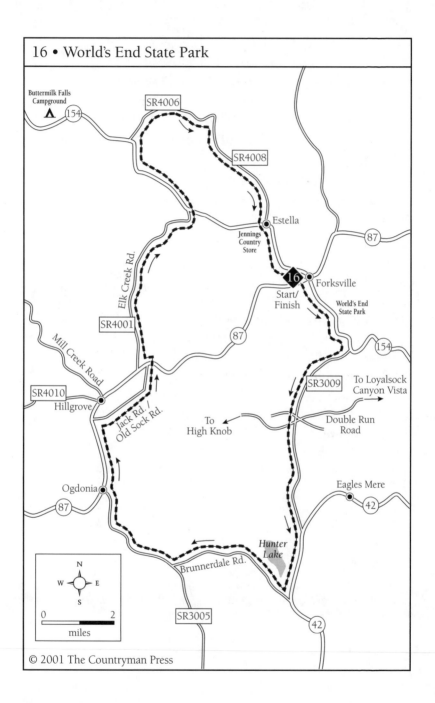

16 • World's End State Park

Buttermilk Falls
Campground

154

SR4006

SR4008

Estella

Jennings
Country
Store

87

16

Forksville

Start/
Finish

World's End
State Park

154

Elk Creek Rd.

SR4001

87

SR3009

To Loyalsock
Canyon Vista

Mill Creek Road

To
High Knob

Double Run
Road

SR4010

Hillgrove

Jack Rd. /
Old Sock Rd.

Ogdonia

87

Eagles Mere

42

N
W   E
S

Hunter
Lake

0   2
miles

Brunnerdale Rd.

SR3005

42

© 2001 The Countryman Press

16
World's End State Park

Distance: *39 miles*

Difficulty: *Moderate*

Terrain: *A few hills and two long climbs. The first is a 3.2-mile climb of 800 feet on SR 3009, from miles 2.2 to 5.4. The second is a 1.6-mile climb of 500 feet on PA 154 from miles 26.9 to 29.5. Several sections of this ride are over hard-packed gravel roads or paved roads with gravel on top. Roads are in good repair. More suitable to a hybrid or mountain bike.*

Location: *30 miles northeast of Williamsport on PA 87, 200 miles northwest of Philadelphia, 150 miles northwest of Allentown, 120 miles north of Harrisburg, and 120 miles west of Scranton.*

Of Special Interest: *In addition to the scenery along the routes, the views from Loyalsock Canyon Vista and High Knob Overlook are rewarding. The roads to both Canyon Vista and High Knob are off SR 3009 at 5.1 miles.*

The Loyalsock Trail passes through World's End State Park. This is a hiking trail almost 60 miles long that crosses the Endless Mountains. It is a wilderness path and there are no facilities on the trail itself. While much of the route travels along ridges, there are several steep climbs. It has many spectacular vistas and is a popular back-packing route. More information is available at the state park office.

Services: *World's End State Park is at 1.8 miles. There is a 70-site campground and 19 rustic cabins available all year. A food concession operates from Memorial Day to Labor Day. The park office has helpful rangers, displays on local wildlife, a small selection of gifts, and public toilets.*

There are also toilets at 5.1 miles in the parking area for High Knob and Loyalsock trailheads, and at the boat launch at Hunter Lake, 10.9 miles.

The Forksville General Store and Eatery is a good place to have breakfast before starting your ride. The phone number is 570-924-4982. At 41.6 miles you can get pizza or other snacks at Jennings Country Store.

The town of Eagles Mere, about 1 mile off the route at 7.9 miles, has many travelers' facilities including small hotels and guest houses, food stores, and restaurants.

Buttermilk Falls Kampground is on PA 154, Ellington Road, in Shunk, about 2 miles off the route at 29.7 miles; 570-924-3427.
Bicycle Shop: *Eagles Mere Mountain Bikes; 570-525-3368.*

To Get There

Take PA 87 North from Williamsport about 30 miles to Forksville. Turn right on PA 154. After 0.25 mile, turn right on Bridge Street and cross the covered bridge. Park at or near the Forksville General Store and Eatery.

World's End State Park, covering 780 acres, is beautiful, relatively undeveloped, and remote. The back roads on this route are lovely all year and breathtaking in the fall. The area is also especially beautiful in June, when the mountain laurel is in bloom.

The name came from the first Europeans to cross this section of the Endless Mountains. Part of the trail clung to the side of a cliff with a steep dropoff to one side. Many early travelers were sure they would plunge into the canyon below, and reach the end of their world.

The Civilian Conservation Corps (CCC) developed the park in the 1930s. The CCC was formed by Franklin D. Roosevelt to "put America back to work." Hundreds of thousands of young men and World War I veterans were hired to clear and develop land for public use. The CCC provided an opportunity to learn skills, gain experience, and earn money that was not otherwise available during the Great Depression. The men built roads, trails, and buildings, cleared brush, planted windbreaks, drained wetlands, and performed many other tasks. Most of the public buildings in the Endless Mountains were built by the CCC, as were many others across the United States.

The Ride

0.0 Start on Bridge Street at PA 154. Turn right on PA 154.

1.8 On the left is the entrance to World's End State Park.

The park office and cabins are located here. Camping sites are farther along PA 154.

2.2 Right on State Road 3009 (SR 3009) and follow Double Run Road toward the town of Eagles Mere.

The first 3.2 miles of SR 3009 is this ride's first climb. At 5.1 miles, a crossroad leads to Loyalsock Creek Canyon View to the left and High Knob to the right. There is a parking area and public toilets at the intersection of SR 3009 and High Knob Road.

You will reach the summit at about 5.5 miles.

7.9 Right on PA 42 at the T. To reach Eagles Mere, turn left.

The town is about a mile away.

9.8 Right at the island on Brunnerdale Road, following Trout Run.

Parts of this road have hard-packed gravel surfaces in good repair.

11.0 The dam and boat launch on Hunter Lake are on the right.

To the left is a parking lot and toilets.

14.0 Brunnerdale Road is joined from the left and becomes SR 3005.

17.0 Right at the T on PA 87 in Ogdonia.

18.9 Right on Old Sock Road and follow Loyalsock Creek.

Old Sock Road is also called Jack Road and Township 350 (T 350).

21.2 Left at the T on PA 87.

21.8 Right on SR 4001 continuing to follow Loyalsock Creek.

If you continue straight on PA 87 for about a mile you will arrive in Hillsgrove, where there is a country store.

22.3 SR 4001 is also called Elk Creek Road.

26.9 Left at the T where Elk Creek Road joins PA 154.

29.5 PA 154 bends to the left as T 411 comes in from the right.

Continue to follow PA 154.

Loyalsock Creek as seen from PA 154.

29.7 Right on SR 4008.

If you continue straight on PA 154 for another 2 miles or so, you will arrive at Buttermilk Falls Kampground in the town of Shunk. The first 1.6 miles of SR 4008 is your second climb. At about 30.6 miles you will reach a plateau at the summit and be rewarded with some extensive views of the area.

31.0 SR 4006 joins SR 4008 from the left. Continue on SR 4008.

32.7 Right to stay on SR 4008 at Eldersville Road.

33.5 Again, turn right to stay on SR 4008. At 33.6 miles continue straight to stay on SR 4008 at McCarthy Road.

36.3 Left at the T on PA 154 in Estella.

Jennings Country Store is located at this intersection.

38.3 Right at the T on PA 87. Cross the first bridge over Little Loyalsock Creek at 38.4 miles.

38.4 Left on PA 154 before 2nd bridge over Loyalsock Creek.

Harold "Red" Grange, a member of both the College and Pro Football Halls of Fame, was born in Forksville in 1903. He played for the Chicago Bears from 1925 to 1936 and was nicknamed "The Galloping Ghost." Although Grange and his family moved to Illinois when he was only five, Forksville is very proud of its native son, and you will see a historic marker on the left on PA 154, detailing his accomplishments.

38.6 Right on Bridge Road.

38.8 End at the Forksville General Store and Eatery.

Linking Routes

For directions on linking the rides in chapters 15, 16, and 17, see page 146.

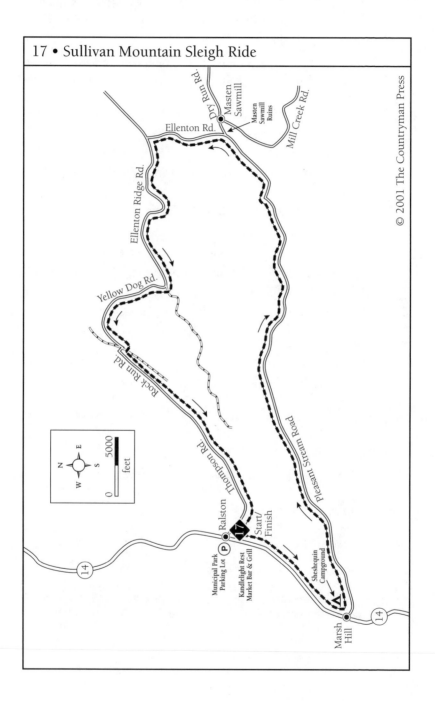

© 2001 The Countryman Press

Dry Run Rd.

Masten
Sawmill

Masten
Sawmill
Ruins

Mill Creek Rd.

Ellenton Rd.

Ellenton Ridge Rd.

Yellow Dog Rd.

Rock Run Rd.

Pleasant Stream Road

Thompson Rd.

N
W   E
S

5000
feet
0

Ralston

17

Start/
Finish

Municipal Park
Parking Lot   P

Kandlelight Rest
Market Bar & Grill

Sheshequin
Campground

14

14

Marsh
Hill

17
Sullivan Mountain Sleigh Ride

Distance: 23 miles
Difficulty: Moderate
Terrain: Unpaved on gravel roads. Gradual climb of 800 feet in 10 miles from 3 miles to 12 miles. A steeper climb of 600 feet in 2 miles follows from 12 to 15 miles. There is an 8-mile downhill that is steep at times. This ride is more suitable to a hybrid or mountain bike. You should have some previous experience with unpaved roads before you try this ride.
Location: 25 miles north of Williamsport, 170 miles northwest of Philadelphia, 115 miles northwest of Allentown, 85 miles north of Harrisburg, and 85 miles west of Scranton.
Services: In addition to the Kandlelight Restaurant, there is a small market and a bar and grill in Ralston immediately after turning off PA 14 on the right. There are no other facilities on the route, so bring food and beverages with you.

To Get There

Take I-180 in Williamsport to US 15 North. Continue north on US 15 to PA 14 North which will take you to Ralston. Take a right at the Kandlelight Restaurant at Thompson Road. At the T in about 0.1 mile, go left, still on Thompson Road. Park in the lot adjacent to the small municipal park just before the bridge that crosses the creek.

This is a great ride if you enjoy a fast downhill run through the woods on unpaved roads. Be sure your brakes are in good working order and you are comfortable handling gravel.

The small, mostly unpaved roads along this route are active logging roads. Well, *active* is an exaggeration. A few trucks climb through the area from time to time. Most likely you will encounter only one or two even if you take the whole day to ride the route. However, since loggers need the roads, they are kept in good condition. They are graded regularly and potholes are filled quickly. The first leg is along the aptly named Pleasant Stream, where there are pretty views and deep woods. This area is a popular choice for remote, rustic vacation cabins, and you will see a few of these scattered along the ride.

The Ride

0.0 *Start by retracing your route back out to PA 14 and turn left.*

2.8 *Left into the town of Marsh Hill on Pleasant Stream Road. There is a sign on PA 14 for Sheshequin Campground. Cross over Lycoming Creek.*

After leaving town you will start to ascend gently, and you will be treated to many lovely views of the stream on your right. At around 10 miles a section of flat, smooth rocks makes a nice spot for a swim on a hot day.

12.2 *Follow the main road to the left.*

This is the site of the Masten Sawmill, a logging town from 1900 to 1930. It was a Civilian Conservation Corps (CCC) camp from 1933 to 1940. During the Great Depression, the United States government hired young men in their teens and 20s who had few or no job skills. Experienced forestry workers and retired military officers were hired to teach the young men skills they could use to earn a living when they left the CCC. The CCC was discontinued when the United States entered World War II.

A hard right leads down to the ruins of the Masten Sawmill. Less than 0.1 mile off the route, this makes a good choice for a picnic lunch. It also gives you a chance to take a break before continuing uphill.

Back on the route, Pleasant Stream Road becomes Ellenton Road, although there are no sign posts until farther up the hill. You will pass pine trees on both sides of the road, planted in perfect lines for erosion control by the CCC. As you come to these

The summit of Ellenton Road

trees, the hill becomes steeper. Cleared farmland provides lovely views of the valley to the east and north where the road flattens out for a bit.

13.7 *Take a hard left onto Ellenton Ridge Road where the main road goes straight. There is a signpost. You will ride up a steep short hill.*

The main road continues to the village of Ellenton and then on to Shunk. This is the linker route to the north section of the World's End Route. See Option Two in the Linker Routes section.

16.9 *The main road turns to the right and becomes Yellow Dog Road. Rock Run Vista is ahead in 3.5 miles.*

It is downhill to the vista, but there is no outlet, and you will have no choice but to climb back to this point.

You are now past the summit of this route and are about to begin the sleigh ride down the mountain. You will descend 1,000 feet in 1.5 miles. Follow the main road and cross Rock Run immediately after passing a small parking lot. Continue going down, although not as steeply. Enter Tiadaghton State Forest and MacIntyre Wildlife Area.

23.4 *End at the parking lot.*

Linking Routes

You can spend several days bicycling around this area by linking the rides in chapters 15, 16, and 17. An easy way to link Sullivan Mountain Sleigh Ride and World's End State Park is through the Masten Sawmill site and the town of Hillsgrove.

At 12.2 miles on the Sullivan Mountain ride, go straight on Pleasant Stream Road instead of turning left on Ellenton Road. Immediately after crossing the stream, make a hard, backward right on Mill Creek Road. After about 10 miles, this unpaved, hard-packed downhill run will take you to the town of Hillsgrove on PA 87. Turn left in Hillsgrove on PA 87. After a mile, turn left on SR 4001 to join the World's End route at 21.8 miles.

A second link between these two routes is a little farther away. At 13.7 miles on the Sullivan Mountain ride, go straight instead of turning left on Ellenton Ridge Road. This will take you into the town of Ellenton in 1.2 miles. At the T, turn right on SR 1015/SR 4003 to Shunk and Tomkins Corner. In Tomkins Corner, at 2.2 miles go straight on SR 4002 to Shunk. The Buttermilk Kampground is in Shunk. Join PA 154 and SR 4006 at 4.9 miles and cross Hoagland Creek. At 6.4 miles, go straight where SR 4006 leaves PA 154. At 8.5 miles, bear left on SR 4008 to join the World's End route at 31 miles.

The town of Hillsgrove also provides a link between the World's End route and the Foothills ride out of Faxon. SR 4010 is 0.25 mile south of Mill Creek Road. Take this road west. When you enter Lycoming County, SR 4010 becomes SR 1005.

Turn right on SR 1006 in Proctor at 6 miles. Go straight on SR 1003 in Wallis Run at 10.4 miles. At 11.5 miles, bear left and join the Foothills ride on SR 1003 at 19.2 miles.

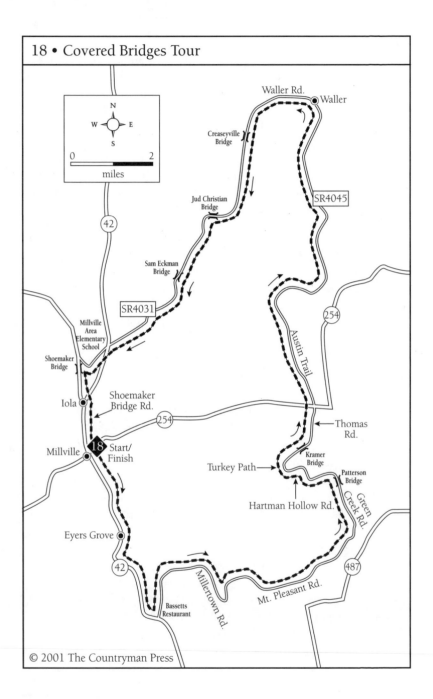

N
W · E
S

0   2
miles

42

Waller Rd.
Waller

Creaseyville
Bridge

SR4045

Jud Christian
Bridge

Sam Eckman
Bridge

SR4031

254

Millville
Area
Elementary
School

Shoemaker
Bridge

Iola

Shoemaker
Bridge Rd.

254

Austin Trail

Thomas
Rd.

Kramer
Bridge

Turkey Path

Patterson
Bridge

Millville

18 Start/
Finish

Hartman Hollow Rd.

Green
Creek Rd.

Eyers Grove

42

Millertown Rd.

Mt. Pleasant Rd.

487

Bassetts
Restaurant

© 2001 The Countryman Press

18
Covered Bridges Tour

Distance: *38 miles*

Difficulty: *Difficult*

Terrain: *Rolling with 4 climbs. There are three 400-foot climbs. The first is from 4.7 to 6.6 miles, the second is from 13 to 14.7 miles, and the third is from 17.6 to 21 miles. The last climb is over 550 feet from 21.5 to 26.3 miles.*

> *Several portions of this route are on unpaved roads. Turkey Path, at 14.7 miles is rough. It is best suited for a hybrid or mountain bike.*

Location: *Millville is about 30 miles southeast of Williamsport, 150 miles northwest of Philadelphia, 100 miles northwest of Allentown, 65 miles north of Harrisburg, and 50 miles west of Scranton.*

Of Special Interest: *Ricketts Glen State Park, about 30 miles northeast of Millville, is one of the most beautiful state parks in Pennsylvania. In the Glens Natural Area, the 7-mile Falls Trail winds down Kitchen Creek past 22 named waterfalls. It became a Registered National Natural Landmark in 1969. Two branches of Kitchen Creek cut deep gorges through Ganoga Glen and Glen Lehigh and join at Waters Meet. From there the creek flows through Ricketts Glen past giant pines, hemlocks, and oaks. Many trees are over 500 years old with diameters of over 5 feet. Some trees are as old as 900 years old. Southern and northern hardwood regions overlap here resulting in a great variety of trees.*

> *You can take a shorter trail of about 0.5 mile, the Evergreen Trail, to see the final series of falls and giant hemlocks and pines.*

Services: *There are a few places to eat in Millville. On PA 42, State Street, you will find the Quakerette Restaurant, the Village Coffee House, and the Original Italian Pizza Place just north of the intersection with PA 254, Main Street. Bassett's Restaurant is on PA 42 at mile 4.7. Pop's*

Quality Market is on PA 254, Main Street, southwest of PA 42.
Fran's Dairy Bar and Restaurant is also in Iola.
The Shady Rest Campground is in Eyers Grove, 2.3 miles south of the start of the ride. A better place to camp, although farther away, is Ricketts Glen State Park. You can also rent cabins, although you must have reservations in advance.
Bicycle Shop: *The closest bicycle shop is about 6 miles south of Millville on PA 42 in Bloomsburg. The Dutch Wheelman Bicycle Shop is at 59 East Main Street, Bloomsburg, PA 17815; 570-784-6524.*

To Get There

From exit 34 on I-80, go north on PA 42 for 8 miles to Millville. There are side streets on both sides of the intersection of PA 42 and PA 254, Main Street, where you can park.

This ride starts in the town of Millville in north central Pennsylvania. The route passes six covered bridges as it meanders around the creeks in the area.

There are a few climbs on this route. Some are steep at times, and one is quite long. But the scenery here is lovely. The farmland is rolling and lightly wooded. The covered bridges are nicely situated on roads with little traffic. Plan to take most of the day, enjoy a picnic lunch, and savor the quiet beauty.

Covered bridges were first constructed in 14th-century central Europe. The abundance of wood in America made covered bridges a logical choice here during the 18th and 19th centuries. The wooden cover kept the bridge surface dry, making it safer and more pleasant, and also protected the bridge and prolonged its life.

The first known covered bridge in North America was 550 feet long and spanned the Schuylkill River in Philadelphia. It was not originally intended to be covered, but a local landowner, hoping to make the bridge more attractive, suggested that it be covered and painted. The popularity of the finished bridge encouraged communities all over the country to begin constructing their own versions. At the peak of their popularity just before the Civil War, Pennsylvania had over 1,500 covered bridges, more than any other state.

The Sam Eckman Covered Bridge was built in 1876.

The Ride

0.0 *Start in Millville at the intersection of PA 42 and PA 254, going south on PA 42.*

Millville was established in 1772 as a Quaker village.

4.7 *Left on Robbins Road, SR 4015/T 600, at Bassett's Restaurant. Cross Little Fishing Creek.*

After crossing the creek you will climb uphill.

5.5 *Right on T 545, an unpaved road in good condition.*

Continue to climb up this very pretty country road.

6.6 *Right at the T on Millertown Road, SR 4011. This road is paved and downhill.*

7.5 *Left on Mount Pleasant Road, SR 4020. Continue to roll down to Fishing Creek.*

10.1 *Left to stay on SR 4020 at the stop sign. Do not cross the bridge. You will follow Fishing Creek, on your right.*

12.0 **Left at the stop sign on SR 4041 at Green Creek Road and Rohrsburg Road.**

13.0 **Left on Hartman Hollow Road, SR 4037.**

You will ride through Patterson, built in 1874.

13.1 **Follow Hartman Hollow Road as it bends to the right.**

The road here is paved but covered with gravel. Go up the hill through lightly wooded farmland.

14.7 **Right on Bowman's Hill Road at this multipoint intersection.**

14.7 **Immediately turn right on Turkey Path.**

This road is unpaved and rough.

15.5 **Go through Kramer Covered Bridge, built in 1881. The road continues to be unpaved up to the T.**

15.7 **Right at the T on Claud Utt Road, T 595. Take an immediate left onto Thomas Road, T 572.**

It looks like you'll be going up the driveway to the farm here, but I promise it really is a road. You will pass several picturesque farms ahead.

16.5 **Right on PA 254 then a quick right on Austin Trail, SR 4039, just past the farmhouse.**

Do not cross Green Creek. You will climb steadily along Little Green Creek. This is a very pretty road.

19.3 **Right on Laudbach Hill Road, T 457.**

Of course a road named Laudbach Hill will involve a climb. This one can be steep at times, but you will reach the summit at about 19.8 miles and then be treated to a downhill coast.

20.4 **Left at the T to join Waller Road, SR 4045. Go straight at 21.6 miles to stay on SR 4045, which becomes Green Creek Road.**

This is the longest climb of the ride, although there are short downhill rests as well. You'll reach the top at the T in Waller.

25.4 **Left on Waller Road, T 720, at the stop sign at the T.**

There is a confusing array of signs at this intersection. This is the theoretical village of Waller. Unityville is to the left in 5 miles. That's where you are going. It is mostly downhill from here to Little Fishing Creek.

25.5 *Bear left to stay on T 720, which is also SR 4032, Creaseyville Road.*

This is a very pleasant section of the route. Don't coast so fast that you miss your turn. Look for Little Fishing Creek.

27.1 *Left on T 710, SR 4031, to follow Little Fishing Creek.*

From here, the route is more down than up, but it rolls up and down quite a bit. The third covered bridge on this route, Creaseyville Bridge, 1881, is to the right, down the hill about 0.3 mile.

29.3 *Bear right downhill to stay on SR 4031.*

You will cross Little Fishing Creek at miles 29.4, 30.5, and 33.2. Jud Christian Covered Bridge, built in 1876, is just off the road to the left at 30 miles. In another mile you will see the Sam Eckman Bridge, also built in 1876, on the right.

You will find the rest of the ride a bit easier with shorter and less steep uphill sections and a couple of fast, easy, downhill coasts.

34.1 *Left at the stop sign on PA 42.*

34.3 *Take the next right on Pine School Road.*

You will pass the Millville Area Elementary School. This section is your last bit of hill climbing. Don't worry, it's like nothing you have done so far.

35.5 *Straight at the stop sign at the intersection of PA 442 and PA 620. Cross PA 442.*

35.5 *Bear left on Chestnut Lane. Immediately bear left on Shoemaker Bridge Road, SR 4027, T 853.*

The bridge is closed to traffic but not to pedestrians.

35.9 *Left at the stop sign at the T on Maple Ridge Road, T 619.*

This is one of the prettiest parts of the route.

36.4 *Left on Legion Road, SR 4027. Cross the bridge into Iola.*

36.6 *Right at the stop sign at the T on PA 42.*

There are a couple of places to eat here, including one that sells ice cream, Fran's Dairy Bar. The last mile to Millville is flat and fast.

37.7 *End at the intersection of PA 42 and PA 254.*

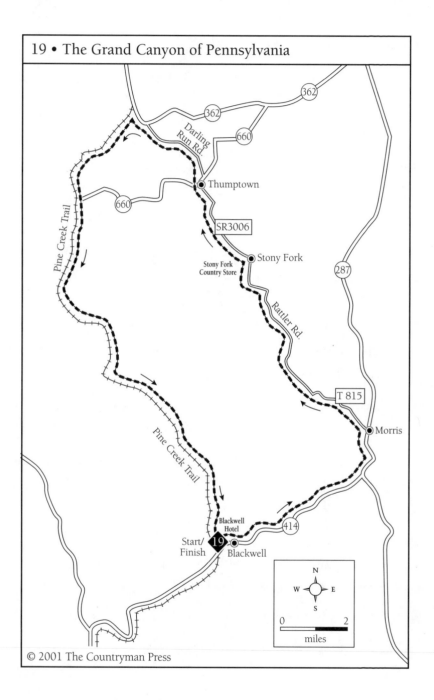

19
The Grand Canyon of Pennsylvania

Distance: 36 miles

Difficulty: Difficult

Terrain: While the last 16 miles are flat to slightly downhill, the first 20 miles are rolling and include two strenuous climbs. Rattler Road climbs 800 feet over 5 miles. From mile 13 to mile 16.5, from the bottom of Rattler Road to the town of Thumptown, you will climb 300 feet.

Most of the roads are paved, but the Pine Creek Trail is gravel, making this ride more suitable to a hybrid or mountain bike.

Location: Blackwell, about 65 miles north of Williamsport, 240 miles northwest of Philadelphia, 180 miles northwest of Allentown, 155 miles north of Harrisburg, and 155 miles west of Scranton.

Of Special Interest: Pine Creek offers excellent opportunities for rafting and canoeing. There are several outfitters that provide guides and equipment for many outdoor activities.

Pine Creek Outfitters (570-724-3003) provides guided raft trips and rents rafts, canoes, wetsuits, and bicycles. They have raft trips through flatwater suitable for children and other less-than-fearless types, as well as whitewater rapids. Canyon Cruise Outfitters & Guides (814-435-2969) offers similar services.

Mountain Trail Horse Center, Inc. (1-877-376-5561) offers guided tours on horseback.

It is possible to travel along mountain bike trails for close to a hundred miles and never stray farther than 15 miles from the Blackwell parking area.

There are also many hiking trails in this area. The Mid-State Trail begins in the Pennsylvania Grand Canyon and continues south for over 150 miles. Starting in Blackwell, where this ride begins, you will climb uphill for about 0.3 mile where the trail levels and provides some great views of the Pine Creek Gorge. At about 0.5 mile and 1 mile, you will see two mountain stream waterfalls, passing through a cherry and hemlock forest. The trail is at its best in June when the mountain laurel is in bloom.

Outside magazine selected the West Rim Trail as Pennsylvania's best hiking trail in 1996. It begins 1 mile south of the Blackwell parking lot, continuing south for 30 miles.

The Black Forest Trail is a few miles south, in the village of Slate Run. This trail goes through scenic Slate Run Gorge. This is a very popular backpacking trail with fantastic scenery. It is a challenging route. Overnight camping is permitted in designated areas and by permit only.

There are also hundreds of shorter trails along Pine Creek Gorge, with scenic vistas overlooking Pine Creek. You can get information on these trails at the offices in Colton Point and Leonard Harrison State Parks.

Services: At the starting point, the Blackwell parking area, there are several services. Across PA 414, the Blackwell Hotel (570-353-6820) has a restaurant and rents bicycles. There is a telephone, drinking water, and a toilet next to the parking lot.

In the town of Morris, at 5.2 miles, there is a general store and a couple of restaurants. You will pass the Stony Fork Country Store at 13.9 miles, where you can buy cold drinks, sandwiches, and other snacks.

Leonard Harrison State Park and Colton Point State Park are on opposite sides of the gorge; 570-724-3061. There is overnight camping at both parks. A private campground, Kenshire Kampsite (814-435-6764), is on the west side of Pine Creek Gorge (or is it Pine Kreek Gorge?). Canyon Country Campground (570-724-3818) is located next to Pine Creek Gorge and has cabins as well as campsites.

Wellsboro has many restaurants and options for overnight lodging.
Bicycle Shop: Blackwell Bikes, Inc., Wellsboro; 570-353-2612.

A view of Pine Creek Gorge from the rim.

To Get There

From I-80, go north at exit 31, I-180, about 25 miles to US 15 in Williamsport. After about 25 miles, go west on PA 414 in Liberty. Blackwell is about 15 miles west of Liberty. Turn left into the Blackwell Access Parking Lot for Pine Creek Trail.

Pine Creek Gorge, called the Grand Canyon of Pennsylvania, is 47 miles long and 1,450 feet at its deepest point. While it is nowhere near the size of Arizona's Grand Canyon, it is still impressive, and it was designated a National Natural Landmark in 1968. The Pine Creek Trail was constructed on an old railway bed. The first segment was opened in 1996. It is about 19 miles long, traveling from Ansonia to Blackwell. This ride begins in Blackwell and climbs up through woods and farmland to the Darling Run Access point, about 1.2 miles south of Ansonia. There you will enjoy a gentle downhill ride on the gravel trail back to Blackwell.

The Ride

0.0 *From the Blackwell Access parking area, turn right onto PA 414, going north.*

The Blackwell Hotel and Bike Rentals are on the left. You will follow Babb Creek. At about 1 mile, look to the left for a small, private cable car that crosses the creek to a home on the opposite side.

5.2 *Left on PA 287 North and PA 414 East at the T and stop sign in Morris.*

There is a post office, a couple of restaurants, and a general store in this area before you cross the creek at 6.1 miles. The Twin Streams Campground is on the left at 6.2 miles. They have a public laundry. Cross the creek again before turning on Rattler Road.

6.3 *Left on Rattler Road, T 815. This is an 800-foot climb for about 5 miles.*

11.3 *Rattler Road bends to the left and then is joined by West Hill Road from the right.*

Continue on Rattler Road. This is the top of your climb, and you will be rewarded by some nice views.

12.1 Right to stay on LR 58012, Rattler Road.

13.0 Right at the T and stop sign to stay on Rattler Road, LR 58012. Join the main road here.

At 13.7 miles, just before you turn, Stony Fork Country Store is on the left. You can get sandwiches and drinks here.

13.8 Left on SR 3006.

Follow the signs for the winding roads, next 2.75 miles. You will climb for about 300 feet from here to Thumptown at 16.5 miles.

15.7 Left to stay on SR 3006. Kendrick Road is straight ahead.

16.5 Right on PA 660 in Thumptown.

16.7 Left on Darling Run Road, T 446. Darling Run Road is gravel covered.

17.4 Straight and then bear left immediately to stay on Darling Run Road where it crosses Stowell Road.

The road deteriorates to dirt and stone here.

19.4 Left at the T to join PA 362.

19.8 Left into the Pine Creek Trail Darling Point Parking Area.

There is water, a telephone, and toilets here.

19.9 Left on to the Pine Creek Trail, heading south.

There are designated camping areas at intervals along the trail. You must have a permit, which is available in Wellsboro. You will share the trail with a few cars at a couple of places where there are parking lots. These are access points to the trail. There are many hiking trails through the woods throughout the area. The trailheads are marked. You can get maps at the state park offices.

35.8 Right onto PA 414. Immediately turn left into the parking area.

VII
PENNSYLVANIA DUTCH
COUNTRY

Pennsylvania Dutch Country

The descendants of the first European settlers in central Pennsylvania, especially Lancaster County, are often referred to as Pennsylvania Dutch. However, their forebears were from Germany, not Holland. English-speaking immigrants who followed converted "Deutsch" to "Dutch."

The designation Pennsylvania Dutch apparently now includes other early European immigrants and their descendents, but the best known are the "plain people." The Amish, Mennonites, and Brethren are three separate religions, but they are all Anabaptists, a Christian sect formed in Europe during the Reformation. The central tenet of Anabaptist religion is that only adults who have professed their faith in Jesus as the son of God should be baptized, and that baptized Christians should remain apart from society at large.

A Catholic priest named Menno Simons joined the Anabaptists in 1536 and united many smaller sects with his charismatic leadership and inspirational writings. His followers were called Mennonites. In 1693, a Swiss bishop named Jacob Amman split from the group; his followers became known as the Amish. Despite this split and others that followed, all Mennonites, Amish, and Brethren share the same basic Anabaptist beliefs. However, they vary considerably in their use of technology, mode of dress, language, and religious practice.

Anabaptists were persecuted in Europe, and they welcomed William Penn's "holy experiment" of religious tolerance in North America, arriving in Lancaster County by the 1720s.

You will see many Amish and Mennonite farms on these rides. You may get the opportunity to speak with some of the farmers and their families. Remember that their plain clothing and modest manner reflect their religious beliefs. They are not performing, nor are they wearing costumes. Respect their privacy, and if you want to take a photograph, ask permission first. Some religions forbid photography, and even if it is allowed, no one likes being treated as scenery.

20
Scenic Octoraro Creek

Distance: 27 miles

Difficulty: Moderate

Terrain: Rolling, with one long climb of 400 feet in 3.5 miles on Puseyville/Bartville Road, from 15.5 miles to 19 miles. Suitable for any bicycle.

Location: Christiana, Pennsylvania, 4 miles south of Gap, 30 miles west of Philadelphia, 50 miles southwest of Allentown, 90 miles east of Harrisburg, and 130 miles south of Scranton.

Of Special Interest: Octoraro Creek was included in the Pennsylvania Scenic Rivers program in 1983. This classification puts the creek under the protection of the Department of Conservation and Natural Resources (DCNR). The DCNR's intention is to "preserve the primitive qualities, the natural and aesthetic values," and to "protect the existing character" of the creek.

Services: There is a pizza restaurant and deli on Gay Street, one block from Bridge Street. The Hershey Market is on Bridge Street at Gay Street. There are no other services along the route, so be sure to bring enough food and water for the whole ride.

Spruce-Edge Farm Guesthouse (717-529-3979) is in Christiana. There are also hotels and restaurants in Gap, about 4 miles north. You will find many choices on PA 41 between Christiana and US 30.

Bicycle Shops: The closest bike shops are in Lancaster. Try the Lancaster Bicycle Shop at 1138 Mannheim Pike, Lancaster; 717-299-9445.

The Lancaster Bicycle Club (717-396-9299) has a nice collection of rides in Lancaster County. They can also provide other information for the cyclist about the area. Their mailing address is P.O. Box 535, Lancaster, PA 17608-0535.

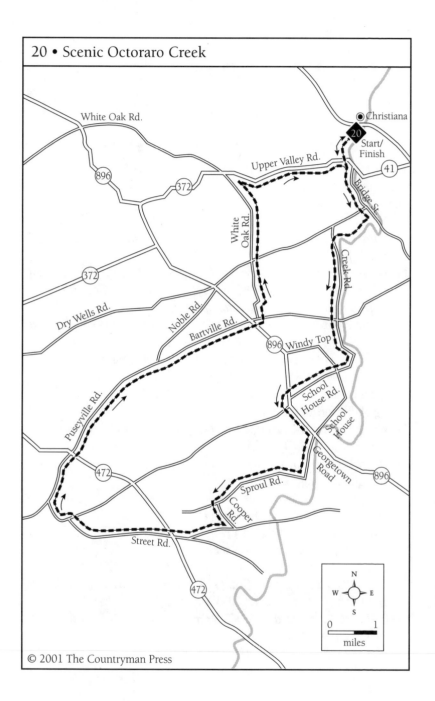

White Oak Rd.

896

372

Upper Valley Rd.

Christiana

20

Start/
Finish

41

Bridge St.

372

White Oak Rd.

Creek Rd.

Dry Wells Rd.

Noble Rd.

Bartville Rd.

896 Windy Top

School House Rd.

School House

Puseyville Rd.

472

Georgetown Road

896

Sproul Rd.

Cooper Rd.

Street Rd.

472

N
W E
S

0   1
miles

To Get There

Follow US 30 West from Philadelphia or US 30 East from Lancaster to Gap, Pennsylvania. Go south on PA 41. Turn right on Newport Avenue, following signs for PA 372, into Christiana. Turn right on Sadsbury Avenue and follow as it turns to the left and becomes Bridge Street.

The ride begins at the traffic light at the intersection of Bridge, Water, and Gay Streets. Hershey's Market is on the left just before the stop sign. Gay Street is to the left. Water Street is PA 372 West angling to the right. Bridge Street continues straight ahead and goes to PA 372 East. Park on the street near the intersection.

The first ride follows scenic Octoraro Creek from Christiana to the south. Creek Road is lovely and wooded, with enough shade to cool even the hottest day. However, by the time you climb Bartville Road, there will be no shade trees to keep the sun off your shoulders. Carry extra water and use your sunscreen liberally.

The Ride

0.0 *Start at the intersection of Bridge, Gay, and Water Streets. Head south on Bridge Street.*

There is a small park with benches and a small parking area on the right at 0.1 mile.

0.2 *Left to stay on Bridge Street where it joins PA 372 East.*

0.5 *Right to stay on Bridge Street where PA 372 turns left and crosses Pine Creek.*

You will quickly find yourself riding through sparsely populated woods. Pass Upper Valley Road at 0.7 mile. Go under the railroad bridge. Pass Lower Valley Road at 0.8 mile.

1.3 *Left at the T on Creek Road where the main road turns right and becomes Noble Road. There is no signpost at this intersection.*

1.5 *Right at the Y to enter Scenic Octoraro Creek.*

You will follow the creek as it meanders to the south along this beautiful road.

There is a buffalo ranch on School House Road just after you leave Creek Road. This photo was taken in the summer, when they lose most of their fur.

1.9 *Bear right to continue on Creek Road. Do not cross the creek.*

4.6 *Left at the T to continue on Creek Road, State Road 2017 (SR 2017). The road to the right is Brick Mill Road, T 391.*

6.1 *Straight ahead on School House Road. Creek Road goes to the left, and Windy Top Road is to the right.*

Yes, those are buffalo on your right just past this intersection. There are many large farms in this area. Amish farmers, who use century-old equipment and techniques, own many of them.

7.1 *Left at the T on PA 896, Georgetown Road.*

8.0 *Right on Sprout Road, SR 2012. Creek Road is to the left. Cross Bell Road, SR 2013, at 9.8 miles.*

10.9 *Left on Cooper Drive, a tiny paved road winding through the farm fields.*

11.6 *Right at the T and stop sign on Street Road, SR 2008.*

Pass a church on the right and go straight across Kirkwood Road, PA 472, in the town of Union at 12.8 miles.

15.8 *Right at stop sign and T on SR 2010, Puseyville Road. To the left is Octoraro Scenic River System. You are back into the woods.*

That long climb you've been looking forward to begins along this road. Cross PA 472, Kirkwood Road, again at 16.5 miles.

17.2 *Go straight across Pumping Station Road.*

The name of the road changes to Bartville Road, SR 2015. The top of the hill, about 19 miles, is wide open. You'll feel like an ant on a bald head.

19.4 *Straight on Bartville Road where the main road turns left to follow Noble Road.*

21.5 *Go straight across PA 896, Georgetown Road.*

21.6 *Next left on White Oak Road.*

This paved road twists through a small residential area.

23.9 *Right on Upper Valley Road after the railroad tracks.*

This will take you into the homes on the outskirts of Christiana. You will climb up a hill, much shorter than the Puseyville Road stretch. Then you will have a relaxing downhill run into Christiana.

26.3 *Left on Bridge Street.*

26.4 *Bear left to join PA 372.*

26.7 *Right to stay on Bridge Street where it leaves PA 372.*

26.9 *End at the intersection of Bridge and Gay Streets.*

Linking Routes

White Oak Road intersects with the Amish Farmland ride (chapter 21) between Noble and Upper Valley Roads. To join the two routes, take a left on Noble Road at 22.1 miles to join the Amish Farmland ride at 19.5 miles. You can detour into Quarryville at 27.1 miles by turning right on US 222. Or you can just keep going by jogging to the right on US 222 and then immediately back to the left on Scotland Road. At White Oak Road and Upper Valley Road at 18.3 miles, turn left on Upper Valley Road and continue to follow this route as described above. The total distance for this longer route is about 54 miles.

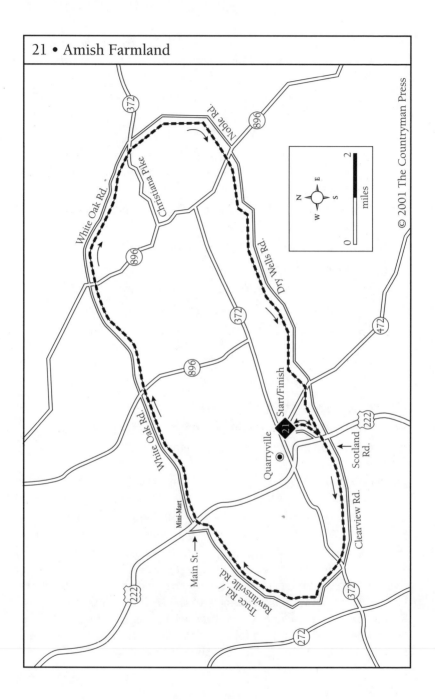

© 2001 The Countryman Press

372

Noble Rd.

896

Christiana Pike

White Oak Rd.

896

miles

N
W · E
S

0   2

472

372

Dry Wells Rd.

896

896

372

White Oak Rd.

Start/Finish

21

222

Scotland Rd.

Quarryville

Mini-Mart

Clearview Rd.

Main St.

222

Truce Rd. / Rawlinsville Rd.

372

272

21
Amish Farmland

Distance: 28 miles

Difficulty: Moderate to Difficult

Terrain: Hilly with one long climb of 540 feet from the turn onto White Oak Road at 14.8 miles to about 18 miles. All roads are paved. Suitable for any type of bicycle.

Location: Quarryville, Pennsylvania, 16 miles southeast of Lancaster, 45 miles west of Philadelphia, 65 miles southwest of Allentown, 75 miles east of Harrisburg, and 120 miles south of Scranton.

Of Special Interest: The common myth is that the Amish do not change with time and do not accept any modern technology. The reality is that change is accepted but only after it is thoroughly discussed. The group must reach consensus that the change will have no negative effects and that any advantages will be truly helpful. Any changes must also not interfere with their religious beliefs. This policy has kept the Amish separate from the world at large, which is in keeping with their religious views, and it has created a very strong community.

Services: There is a minimart at 15 miles, at the intersection of US 222 and White Oak Road, just before your long climb. Kendig's General Store is at the intersection of Noble Road and PA 896 at 19.4 miles.

The Quarryville Family Restaurant is on PA 372, a couple of blocks to the left as you leave the Quarryville Park. Turkey Hill Mini-Market is at the intersection of PA 372 and US 222.

There are three guesthouses in Quarryville: Bright Pine Hollow Farm (717-299-4501); Runnymede Farm Guesthouse (717-786-3625); and Sensenig Bed and Breakfast (717-786-3128).

Bicycle Shop: The closest bike shop is Lancaster Bicycle Shop at 1138 Mannheim Pike, Lancaster, PA 17601; 717-299-9445.

To Get There

Take I-76 to US 222 south. Follow US 222 South through Lancaster. Continue south on US 22 about 16 miles to Quarryville. Turn left where US 222 joins PA 372 and becomes State Street. In about 1 mile, pass the intersection with Church Street where US 222 turns right and goes south. Take the next right off State Street onto Hess Street. Take the second left on Park Avenue and immediately turn right into Quarryville Community Park. Park in the lot straight ahead.

You can also follow PA 372 west from Christiana. When you get to Quarryville, turn left on PA 472. In 0.1 mile, turn right on Park Avenue. The parking area is on the left.

You will begin this ride in the community park in Quarryville. It is a hilly but peaceful ramble through picturesque farmland. As with the Octoraro Creek ride, you will pass several Amish farms.

The Amish dress in modest clothing that they believe encourages humility and separation from the world. Most Amish clothing uses straight pins, hook-and-eye fasteners, or snaps, rather than buttons, which are considered decorative. Dresses are long; suit coats are plain and collarless. Women do not cut their hair, but wear it rolled into a bun, fastened at the back of their heads, and covered with a "prayer covering" made of cotton or netting. Men do not wear mustaches, but grow beards after they marry.

The Ride

0.0 *Start in the parking area of the Quarryville Community Park. Turn left at the park entrance on Park Avenue.*

0.6 *Left on US 222 at the T.*

This road can be busy, but you will turn onto a quiet road soon. There is a good shoulder to ride on.

0.7 *Bear right on Scotland Road.*

Leave the traffic behind and follow this farm road.

1.3 *Right at the Y to stay on Scotland Road.*

1.9 *Right at the Y on Clearview Road.*

You will leave the main road here.

Rolling hills and large Amish farms are features of the countryside

3.6 Cross PA 327. Immediately turn right on Hopkins Mill Road.

5.3 Right at the T on Truce Road/Rawlinsville Road.

These roads were all named for the town they led to. However, if they lead to more than one town, they can have two names. In this case, both Truce and Rawlingsville are to the left.

In about 0.5 mile, you will pass through a small residential area. In less than a mile, you'll be back out in the boonies.

8.0 Left on Main Street.

This is the pretty little town of New Providence.

8.4 Right on US 222.

8.5 Left on White Oak Road. There is a gas station and minimart at this intersection.

This is your long climb. You will reach the summit in about 1.2 miles. The Octoraro Creek ride (chapter 20) intersects with this one on White Oak Road. If you are combining the two routes, you will turn left on Upper Valley Road in 9.8 miles. At that point, switch back to the Octoraro Creek route to finish your ride in Christiana.

12.5 *Jog to the right and then immediately back to the left to stay on White Oak Road at Mount Pleasant Road.*

You will enter a quiet wooded area in about 0.5 mile. On the left in another 0.5 mile, there is a great view of the valley.

14.0 *Go straight through the stop sign at PA 896.*

14.6 *Go straight through the stop sign at Vintage Road.*

This section of White Oak Road is more populated.

17.5 *Cross Christiana Pike, PA 372.*

18.3 *Cross Upper Valley Road.*

This is the turn to Christiana if you have combined this ride with the Octoraro Creek Route.

You climb a short, steep hill at 18.6 miles after crossing the railroad tracks and Valley Run.

19.5 *Right on SR 2009, Noble Road.*

20.4 *Right at the stop sign on PA 896, Georgetown Road.*

Kendig's General Store is on the right.

20.5 *Immediately turn left on Dry Wells Road.*

21.9 *Cross West Octoraro Creek.*

24.4 *Cross Pumping Station Road.*

25.2 *Right to join Hess Road at the T.*

25.3 *Immediately turn left back on Dry Wells Road.*

You are still on the main road here.

25.9 *Cross PA 472, Kirkwood Pike.*

27.1 *Right on US 222.*

This turn is immediately after a cemetery on the right.

27.2 *Next right on Park Avenue.*

27.8 *Right on Memorial Drive into Quarryville Community Park and parking area.*

Linking Routes

For information on linking this ride with chapter 20, see page 167.

VIII
HILLS ALONG THE
SUSQUEHANNA RIVER

Hills along the Susquehanna River

As the name of this section implies, you will do some climbing if you ride these routes. But the scenery makes the work worthwhile, and both routes are short enough that most intermediate cyclists won't find them overly taxing.

The first inhabitants of this area were the Shenk's Ferry Indians. Before the late 16th century they created petroglyphs found on Sculptured Island just below the Holtwood Dam. By the end of the 1500s, Susquehanna Indians, driven south by Iroquois, overtook the Shenk's Ferry culture. A mass grave located in Shenk's Wildflower preserve is believed to be evidence of warfare between the two tribes. The Susquehanna are thought to have led the massacre.

By the late 17th century, the Iroquois deposed the Susquehanna nation. In turn, the Europeans quickly subdued the Iroquois before the start of the 18th century, and their descendants remain dominant today.

The lifestyle and use of the river changed dramatically over the next 200 years as the agrarian economy was replaced by an industrial economy—through the production of electricity. McCall's Ferry Power Company began construction of Holtwood Dam in 1905 where McCall's Ferry operated from 1740 to 1936. In 1910, the Pennsylvania Water and Power Company (PW&P) completed the dam, located upstream of PA 372. In 1955, PW&P merged with Pennsylvania Power and Light (PP&L), which now manages the dam, power plant, and surrounding land. There is also a dam and power plant farther upstream near the town of Safe Harbor, built in 1932 by Safe Harbor Power Company. In 1968, Philadelphia Electric Company, now PECo Energy, built a hydroelectric plant at Muddy Run, where you will ride.

Fortunately, these companies maintain the area for public recreation and preserve the native flora and fauna. The result is thousands of acres of roads and trails with many opportunities to ride, walk, and enjoy natural surroundings.

The Tucquan Creek ride begins near the Pequea Recreational Area and crosses Tucquan Creek and Natural Area on its way to Muddy Run and adjacent Susquehannock State Park. The Conestoga Creek ride begins near the Safe Harbor Power Company. You will follow Conestoga Creek toward Lancaster before turning back to the river.

Linking Routes

For the truly ambitious, these rides can be linked via River Road to create a 54-mile route. At mile 23.2 of the Tucquan Creek route, continue straight on River Road instead of turning on River Hill Road. After 2.6 miles you will arrive at the parking area at the start of the Conestoga Creek ride (chapter 23). Complete all of that ride and double back along River Road over the same 2.6 miles to River Hill Road. Turn right and continue on River Hill Road to the parking area at the start of the Tucquan Creek route.

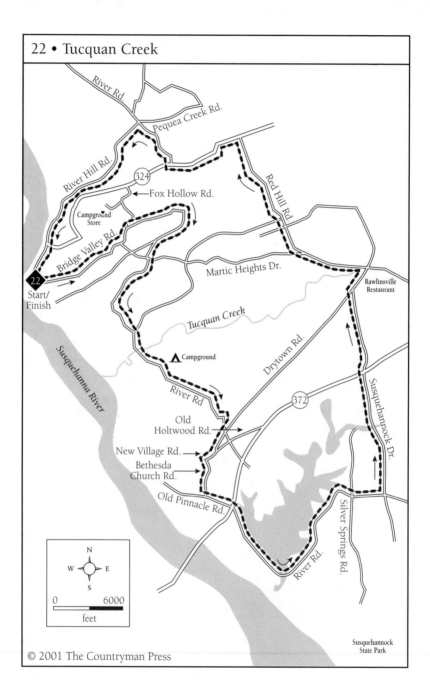

River Rd.

Pequea Creek Rd.

River Hill Rd.

324

← Fox Hollow Rd.

Campground
Store

Red Hill Rd.

Bridge Valley Rd

Martic Heights Dr.

Rawlinsville
Restaurant

22
Start/
Finish

Tucquan Creek

Susquehanna River

▲ Campground

River Rd.

Drytown Rd.

372

Susquehannock Dr.

Old
Holtwood Rd.

New Village Rd.

Bethesda
Church Rd.

Old Pinnacle Rd.

River Rd.

Silver Springs Rd.

N
W E
S

0   6000
feet

Susquehannock
State Park

22
Tucquan Creek

Distance: 26 miles

Difficulty: Moderate to Difficult

Terrain: Hilly throughout. All roads are paved. Suitable for any type of bicycle.

Location: Pequea Recreational Area, Pequea, Pennsylvania, 50 miles west of Philadelphia, 70 miles southwest of Allentown, 70 miles east of Harrisburg, and 150 miles south of Scranton.

Of Special Interest: Shenk's Ferry Wildflower Preserve is a few miles northwest of PA 324 on River Road. Pennsylvania Power & Light (PP&L) also owns this land. The peak months are April and May, when over 130 varieties of wildflowers are in bloom. You cannot ride your bike along the trail—an old railway bed—but it is worth the time to walk.

Services: The name of the Pannebaker Rawlinsville Hotel and Restaurant, at 17.9 miles, is bigger than the place itself. There is no hotel, nor has there ever been one as far as anyone knows. "They've just always called it that." But it is a great place for lunch or dinner. They are open daily.

The Pequea Recreation Area, 86 Fox Hollow Road, Pequea, PA 17565; 717-284-4587, is on PA 324 and Fox Hollow Road, about 2 miles from the starting point of the ride. They have a well-stocked camp store as well as a campground, laundry, showers, and picnic tables. There are playgrounds and organized activities in the summer.

The Tucquan Family Campground is at 6.3 miles.

You will pass Susquehannock State Park at 13.6 miles. There are picnic tables, water, and public toilets. There is also a public toilet in the parking area at the starting point.

There are also several hotels in Lancaster including an Econo

Lodge at 2140 US 30 East; 717-397-1900. Rock-a-Bye Bed and
Breakfast is about 5 miles west of the intersection of US 222 and PA
372, south of Lancaster; 717-872-5990.

Bicycle Shop: The closest bike shop is in Lancaster where there are
several choices. The Lancaster Bicycle Shop, 1138 Mannheim Pike,
Lancaster, PA 17601; 717-299-9445, has a good reputation.

To Get There

From I-76, take US 222 South to US 30. Go west on US 30 about 1 mile
to PA 501. Go south on PA 501 about 1 mile and follow signs to the right
on McGovern Avenue for US 222 South. You will travel through the
city of Lancaster for about 2 miles. Then follow signs for PA 324 South.
Follow PA 324 to its end at the Susquehanna River, about 10 miles. Drive
straight ahead into the public parking lot.

You will work for the views on this route, as it is quite hilly. But there
are nice places to stop for a rest. You will begin in the Pequea Recreational Area, where there are many miles of hiking trails to explore if you
care to spend the time.

The view from Pinnacle Rock, which you will pass at 7.2 miles, is one
of the best in this area. The vista is about 2 miles to the right. From the
pinnacle, trails follow the Susquehanna River to Kelly's Run Recreational Area and beyond.

Susquehannock State Park makes another good place for a picnic
lunch. Or continue to the Pannebaker Rawlinsville Hotel and Restaurant at the ride's summit at 17.9 miles.

The Ride

0.0 *Start in the parking lot on PA 324 and Bridge Valley Road.*

1.3 *Bear left to stay on Bridge Valley Road at Short Road.*

2.0 *Bear left again at Westview Road and reach the top of the
first hill of the ride.*

2.5 *Stay right to stay on Bridge Valley Road where Fox Hollow
Road joins from the left.*

3.5 *Right on River Road. Follow the double yellow lines from here to Drytown Road to stay on River Road.*

4.2 *Bear left at House Rock Road.*

4.5 *Turn left on Clark Hill Road, then a quick right back on River Road.*

Clark Hill Road is the top of your second climb.

5.0 *Bear left again at Delta Road.*

Tucquan Nature Reserve is at 6.1 miles. There are hiking trails and a parking area. Cross Tucquan Creek and the bottom of your downhill run at 6.3 miles and begin to climb again. The Tucquan Family Campground is on the left at 6.6 miles.

Pinnacle Road is to the right at 7.2 miles. There is a great view of the Susquehanna River less than 2 miles along this road. The summit of this climb is at 7.5 miles.

7.8 *Bear right to stay on River Road at McKelvey Lane.*

You'll climb again for 0.5 mile starting at 8.1 miles. But the next 7 miles will be easier.

8.5 *Right on Drytown Road.*

8.8 *Right on Old Holtwood Road.*

This is the Kelly Run Recreational Area, also owned by PP&L.

9.1 *Left on New Village Road.*

9.3 *Stay on the main road where the name changes to Bethesda Church Road.*

9.7 *Left on Old Pinnacle Road.*

10.1 *Bear right at the island to River Road and PA 372.*

10.2 *Cross PA 372, which becomes River Road.*

Cross the dam at Muddy Run at 11.6 miles where the road starts a gentle climb. The entrance to Susquehannock State Park is at 12.6 miles. There are picnic tables, water, and public toilets.

13.6 *Cross Silver Springs Road.*

14.1 *Left at the stop sign on Susquehannock Drive.*

The next hard climb begins at 15.4 miles.

16.1 *Cross PA 372. You will approach PA 372 at an angle and jog*

slightly to the right and left to cross and continue on Susquehannock Drive.

17.5 **Right on Drytown Road.** Built in 1851, the Pannebaker Rawlinsville Hotel and Restaurant is on the left, a nice place to
stop for lunch.

The Rawlinsville Trolley Line ran from 1904 until 1916 along a
6-mile track. It carried hundreds of people up the hill from the
river during camp meeting season.

17.9 **Left on Martic Heights Road.** Klements General Store is on
the right.

18.9 **Bear right at the Y on Red Hill Road,** leaving the main road.

Relax, you'll be riding down Red Hill, not up. Look for the red
road sign. You will enjoy some nice views from up here.

20.3 **Bear left to stay on Red Hill Road at Stump Road.**

20.9 **Bear left again at Lakewood Road.**

21.4 **Bear left at the Y on PA 324, Marticville Road.**

Pass River Road where it enters from the left at 22.1 miles. Cross
the creek.

22.2 **Right on River Road on the other side of the creek.**

23.1 **Bear left at the island to stay on River Road at Pequea Creek
Road.**

23.2 **Left on River Hill Road.**

24.8 **Your last mile is an easy downhill glide.**

25.8 **End at the parking lot on the right at PA 372.**

23
Conestoga Creek

Distance: 23 miles (optional shorter route of 14 miles)
Difficulty: Moderate (shorter route is easy to moderate)
Terrain: Rolling with 2 long climbs (short route has only 1 climb). The
first climb is 300 feet from Central Manor Road, 8.8 miles to 13.8
miles on Schultz Road. The second climb is 350 feet up Turkey Hill on
River Road from miles 17 to 21. All roads are paved and are suitable
for any bicycle.
Location: Safe Harbor Park on River Road, 60 miles west of Philadel-
phia, 70 miles southwest of Allentown, 90 miles east of Harrisburg,
and 150 miles south of Scranton.
Services: There are picnic tables, toilets, and drinking water at the Safe
Harbor Park. You will pass the Manor Bakery and Grill at 10.5 miles.
Mellinger Manor B&B (717-871-0699) is 0.1 mile off the route at
18.7 miles. It is on the shorter route at 10.4 miles.
Bicycle Shop: The closest bike shop is in Lancaster where there are
several choices. The Lancaster Bicycle Shop, 1138 Mannheim Pike,
Lancaster, PA 17601; 717-299-9445, has a good reputation.

To Get There

Follow directions for the Tucquan Creek Ride but turn right on River
Road after about 7 miles on PA 324. From I-76, take US 222 South to US
30. Go west on US 30 about 1 mile to PA 501. Go south on PA 501 about
1 mile and follow signs to the right on McGovern Avenue for US 222
South. You will travel through the city of Lancaster for about 2 miles.
Then follow signs for PA 324 South. Follow PA 324 to its end at the
Susquehanna River, about 10 miles. Drive straight ahead into the public
parking lot. Follow River Road about 2.5 miles. The park is on the left.
In 1632, the King of England deeded Lord Baltimore land north of the

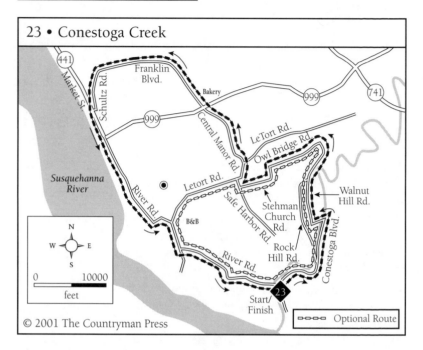

23 • Conestoga Creek

Susquehanna River

© 2001 The Countryman Press

0 — 10000 feet

N
W — E
S

Optional Route

Start/Finish

Chesapeake Bay to the 40th parallel. A plaque in Washington Boro, mile 15, is located at the northern limit of Lord Baltimore's property. Unfortunately, in 1681, land was deeded to William Penn from the 39th to the 42nd parallel. Until the early 1700s, disputes were uncommon because few Europeans settled so far to the west. However by the mid-18th century, violent confrontations over property rights were frequent.

At that point, descendents of William Penn signed an agreement with Charles Calvert, the fifth Lord Baltimore, to adjust the Maryland/Pennsylvania border. The agreement set the western boundary at 39 degrees 43 minutes. Discussion of the survey and other details quickly deteriorated. Bloody encounters between settlers continued until King George II forced both sides into negotiations, allowing a survey to begin in 1750.

It was another 13 years before Charles Mason and Jeremiah Dixon arrived in Philadelphia to survey the final line. The men were known to be excellent astronomers and mathematicians; and in fact, their survey is remarkably accurate even by today's standards. Mason and Dixon finished the survey on September 25, 1766, finally ending the disputes and creating the boundary now known as the Mason-Dixon Line.

In 1820, the Mason-Dixon Line also became the boundary between states in which slavery was allowed and those in which it was illegal. Since that time, the Mason-Dixon Line has been associated with the division of northern and southern states.

The Susquehanna River flows through a narrow pass between high cliffs at Turkey Hill, and then the river becomes wide and slow near the mouth of Conestoga Creek. Here, where boaters pause to rest after negotiating the rapids, is the town of Safe Harbor. In the mid-1800s, Safe Harbor was a major ironworks center. However, floods were common on this low area, and the high water of 1918 destroyed so much of the town that residents moved and businesses closed for good. Since then, Safe Harbor has been a small, quiet village up on the hills above the river.

These shallow marshes are home to thousands of water and predatory birds that live here year-round, including herons, egrets, eagles, hawks, and ospreys. The Susquehanna River Valley is also part of the Atlantic Flyway, the north-south migratory route for hundreds of thousands of birds. The Conejohela Flats, a series of low islands northwest of Safe Harbor, are visited twice a year by tens of thousands of tundra or whistling swans as well as many kinds of ducks, grebes, loons, and several types of swallows, warblers, geese, and gulls.

The Ride

0.0 *Left out of the parking lot of Safe Harbor Park on River Road.*

0.8 *Straight where River Road turns left and crosses the creek.*

Stay on the main road, which becomes Conestoga Boulevard. Conestoga River Park is at this intersection. This is a lovely section following the creek.

3.2 *Left on Stone Hill Road at the first bridge over the creek.*

Cross Conestoga Creek on the metal grate bridge.

3.5 *Right on Rock Hill Road.*

The signpost says that South Creek Road is straight ahead.

4.6 *Straight at the stop sign and join Walnut Hill Road, which comes in from the left.*

Here, you are in the residential outskirts of Lancaster.

5.6 *Left on Owl Bridge Road.*

6.3 *Cross Little Conestoga Creek on Owl Bridge Road.*

Start going uphill. This area is rural, and farms become more numerous.

7.0 *Bear left to stay on Owl Bridge Road at Sheep Lane.*

7.2 *Follow the road to the right to stay on Owl Bridge Road.*

At 7.6 miles, Stehman Church Road joins from the left.

8.2 *Right at the stop sign on Safe Harbor Road.*

8.3 *Letort Road comes in from the right. Safe Harbor Road becomes Letort Road at this point. Follow Letort as it turns to the left in less than 0.1 mile.*

This is where you can take a shorter route. Turn left on Letort Road instead of following the road to the right. Bear left to stay on Letort Road at 9.6 miles. Continue to follow Letort Road, which ends at a T at 10.1 miles. Turn left on Creswell Lane. Turn right on Breneman Road at 10.4 miles. Mellinger Manor B&B is at the corner. At 10.5 miles, turn left on River Road and join the full route at mile 18.7. The total distance of the shorter route is 14.7 miles.

8.8 *Bear left on Central Manor Road.*

9.9 *Bear left and follow the main road, Central Manor Road.*

The smaller road straight ahead is Supervisor Road. Go straight across PA 999, Blue Rock Road at 10.6 miles. The Manor Bakery and Grill is at 10.5 miles.

11.7 *Straight on Franklin Boulevard at the five-point intersection at Moments of Glad Tidings Haverford Church.*

The main road turns right here and follows Habecker Church Road briefly before turning left and becoming Central Manor Road once again.

12.1 *Bear left to stay on Franklin Boulevard at Seitz Road.*

13.5 *Straight on Schultz Road at the stop sign where Franklin Boulevard turns right.*

You are entering the boundary of Washington Boro.

14.5 *Follow the road to the left where it becomes Market Street.*

This is an older, quaint row of homes along the river.

14.9 *Right at the T on Manor Street.*

15.0 *Left on Water Street, PA 441.*

There is a plaque here about the Mason and Dixon Line. This was the northern limit of Lord Baltimore's land before disputes arose with William Penn's descendants.

15.6 *Make a sharp left onto PA 999, and then a quick right which puts you back on River Road.*

At about 17.5 miles, you will begin the hard climb of this route: up Turkey Hill. Cross Letort Road, where the short route joins the long one, at 18.7 miles. You will reach the summit at about 20.2 miles and begin a relaxing downhill ride into Safe Harbor.

22.2 *Cross Conestoga Creek, following River Road as it turns left.*

22.3 *Turn right to stay on River Road at Conestoga Boulevard.*

23.0 *Turn right into the parking area.*

IX
GETTYSBURG, THE TURNING
POINT OF THE CIVIL WAR

Gettysburg

The battle of Gettysburg was pivotal in the Civil War, yet it began with a chance encounter. Confederate troops sent into Gettysburg for supplies happened to spot a forward column of General George G. Meade's Union cavalry on July 1, 1863. The battle began that day and continued until July 3. During that time, more men fought and more men died than in any other North American battle. The conflict involved over 172,000 men, an estimated 500 tons of ammunition, and 634 cannons on 25 square miles of farmland. Ultimately, there were 51,000 casualties.

A critical point of the battle was a courageous and desperate attempt by Confederate soldiers under the command of Major General George E. Pickett to rush the Union defenses. This attack, known as Pickett's Charge, brought 12,000 men across an open field. In less than an hour ,there were 7,500 casualties.

For two more years, the war continued to crush bodies and spirits on both sides until Lee's surrender at Appomattox.

Here are two routes through the town of Gettysburg and the surrounding area. The countryside is picturesque farmland and green, rolling fields. It makes a beautiful and almost incongruous setting for the more than 1,000 monuments on 40 miles of scenic avenues dedicated to those who fought the bloodiest battle of our country's bloodiest war.

The best place to begin your bike ride, or any visit to Gettysburg, is the National Military Park visitors center. However, as I write this book, the military park is preparing to demolish the current visitors center and build a new one a half mile away. No matter what stage the renovations have reached when you visit, there will undoubtedly be public parking somewhere near the current visitors center, a quarter of a mile south of US 15 on PA 134 South. However, since I cannot give you specific instructions at this time, both Gettysburg tours will begin and end at Lincoln Square, the central square of town.

Of Special Interest: *Gettysburg is a very popular destination for tourists. It can be hot, humid, and crowded here in the summer with temperatures in the 90s and 1.5 million visitors annually. But don't let that keep you away. I have made three trips to Gettysburg and I was equally moved and glad each time I came. Try to visit in the spring for the best weather and the smallest crowds.*

The Gettysburg Travel and Convention Center can provide information on restaurants and overnight lodging as well as descriptions of many other attractions in the area. They provide free brochures for several self-guided driving tours. The Scenic Valley Auto Tour is 36 miles long. The Historic Conewago tour is 40 miles and also intended for automobiles. There is also a walking tour of downtown Gettysburg.

In the summer, there are walks, talks, programs, and living history demonstrations at various locations. The visitors center will fill you in. Notable among these attractions is the Cyclorama, a a 360-foot, circular oil painting on canvas of Pickett's Charge, completed in 1884. Admission includes a 20-minute sound and light program, a 20-minute film, and several exhibits. There are also many miles of horse trails and walking trails, from the 1-mile High Water Mark Trail beginning at the Cyclorama, to the 9-mile Billy Yank Trail. There is also a self-guided walking trail through the national cemetery. Again, check at the visitors center.

Dwight D. Eisenhower, 34th president of the United States from 1952 to 1960, chose a farm adjacent to the military park as the site of his home in 1950. He and his wife, Mamie, lived here until 1969, when it was deeded to the U.S. Park Service. Today, the Gettysburg National Military Park maintains the Eisenhower National Historic Site. It is open daily 9–4 from April 1 through October 31, and closed in January and on Mondays and Tuesdays, November through March. There are no parking facilities at the Eisenhower farm, and you may visit only by taking a shuttle bus from the Gettysburg National Military Park visitors center. Admission is charged. Call 717-338-9114 for information.

There are numerous museums in the area, most devoted to military history, especially on the Civil War. Admission is charged for most indoor attractions. There are also many shops that specialize in Civil War-era antiques and memorabilia.

Gettysburg Convention Center and Visitor's Bureau is at 35 Carlisle Street, Gettysburg, PA 17325; 717-334-6274.

Location: Gettysburg is 38 miles southwest of Harrisburg on US 15.

To Get There: Take I-81 to Harrisburg. Then follow US 15 South. This becomes Carlisle Street, which intersects with US 30, Chambersburg Road, at Lincoln Square.

Services: You will find many places for food and overnight accommodations in and around Gettysburg although there are none in the military park itself.

It is always a good idea to make reservations for overnight accommodations. With so many choices, it would be impossible to list them all. However, I will mention the following as places to begin your search.

The Brafferton Inn is one of the most popular B&B's in the area. It is at 44 York Street; 717-337-3423.

For less expensive digs, try the Gettysburg Econo Lodge, 945 Baltimore Pike; 717-334-6715.

There is a youth hostel at 27 Chambersburg Road; 717-334-1020.

If you prefer to camp, the Gettysburg KOA is at 20 Knox Road; 717-642-5713.

Many restaurants line PA 134 (Taneytown Road), US 15 (Steinwehr Avenue, Baltimore Street, and Carlisle Street) and US 30 (Chambersburg Road) as they pass through the town and the park.

The Gettysburg National Military Park visitors center has public parking, toilets, a gift shop, and information on the park and the town.

24
East Cavalry Battlefield

Distance: *43 miles*
Difficulty: *Moderate*
Terrain: *Mostly flat with a 7-mile section of rolling hills and one climb. Suitable for any bicycle.*
Location: *Gettysburg is 38 miles southwest of Harrisburg on US 15.*
Services: *There are no places to buy food or beverages, so be sure to carry enough for the entire route. The East Cavalry Battlefield makes a quiet, lovely place for a picnic at about 10 miles. There are many other pleasant spots along the road.*

To Get There

Take I-81 to Harrisburg. Then follow US 15 South. This becomes Carlisle Street, which intersects with US 30, Chambersburg Road, at Lincoln Square.

On July 3, before Pickett's Charge began, the Union cavalry met the newly arrived Confederate cavalry in the fields to the east of Gettysburg. This ride takes you through the East Cavalry Battlefield after leading you past many farms that were used as makeshift hospitals. There are few tourists along these roads, and you may be the only traveler through much of the route.

The Ride

0.0 Start by heading west from Lincoln Square on Chambersburg Street, US 30.

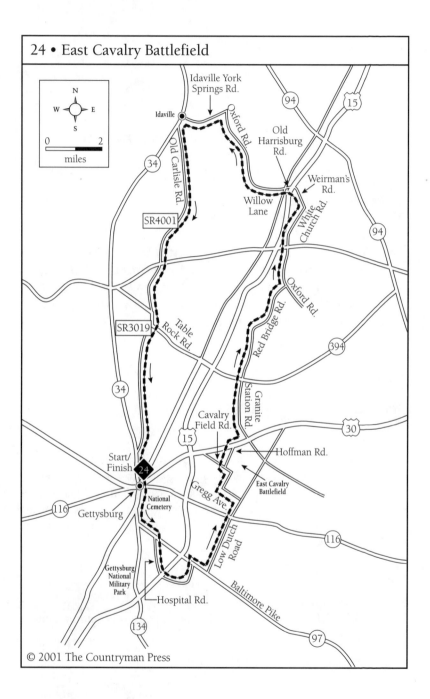

N
W • E
S

0   2
miles

Idaville York
Springs Rd.

Idaville

Oxford Rd.

94

15

Old
Harrisburg
Rd.

Weirman's
Rd.

34

Old Carlisle Rd.

SR4001

Willow
Lane

White Church Rd.

94

Oxford Rd.

SR3019

Table
Rock Rd.

Red Bridge Rd.

394

34

Granite Station Rd.

Cavalry
Field Rd.

Hoffman Rd.

15

30

Start/
Finish

24

East Cavalry
Battlefield

116

Gettysburg

National
Cemetery

Gregg Ave.

Low Dutch Road

116

Gettysburg
National
Military
Park

Hospital Rd.

Baltimore Pike

134

97

© 2001 The Countryman Press

0.1 Left on Washington Street.

0.8 Straight through the traffic light where Washington Street becomes PA 132 South, Taneytown Road.

The crossroad is US 15, Steinwehr Avenue.

The National Cemetery is on the left at 1.0 mile. Almost 7,000 soldiers who died in the battle are buried here along with over 76,000 other U.S. veterans and their dependents. Lincoln's Gettysburg Address was delivered here at the dedication of the cemetery on November 19, 1863. The speech lasted barely two minutes but remains one of the world's most poignant tributes to those who fight and die for a cause. You can take a detour through here on your bike.

The visitors center was located on the right at the time this book was written.

1.3 Left on Hunt Avenue. All park roads, including this one, are closed from 10 PM until 6 AM.

1.8 Right on Baltimore Pike, PA 97.

2.4 Right on Blacksmith Shop Road. MacAllister Road and MacAllister Macduff Adventure Golf are on the left.

2.5 Left at the Y to stay on Blacksmith Shop Road.

2.8 Bear left at the Y on Hospital Road.

Along this road you will see many plaques indicating the location of Civil War field hospitals. Both armies rescued as many of the wounded as they could as they retreated on July 3. However, the remaining able-bodied soldiers were exhausted, supplies were dwindling, carts and wagons were inoperable, and an estimated 5,000 horses lay dead in the fields and woods. Tens of thousands of men, wounded, dead, and dying, were left for the approximately 2,400 townspeople to care for.

3.8 Left on Sachs Road at the T. Cross over US 15 at 3.9 miles.

At 4.5 miles, cross a bridge over Rock Creek. There are more field hospital sites, and the name of the road changes to Goulden Road.

5.2 Left on White Church Road at the stop sign and T.

5.7 Right on Baltimore Pike, PA 97, at the T. Lightner House B&B is on the left at 5.9 miles.

6.2 Left on Low Dutch Road. Cross PA 116, Hanover Road, at 8.5 miles.

9.1 Left on Gregg Avenue into East Cavalry Field.

10.0 Follow the road to the right where it becomes Confederate Cavalry Road.

The cannons on this road were among the 634 used in the battle. At 10.7 miles, the road bends to the left and becomes Cavalry Avenue.

11.0 Right on Hoffman Road at the stop sign.

11.8 Right on York Road, US 30, at the T.

This is a busy road, but there is a good shoulder.

12.3 Left on Granite Station Road.

14.4 Cross PA 394.

The name is Shriver's Corner Road to the left and Hunter's Hampton Road to the right. To make things a little more complicated, once you cross PA 394, the road is called Red Bridge Road. However, the first sign you will see with that name is up the road a bit at 14.5 miles. Go straight to stay on Red Bridge Road at 15.0 miles where Woodside Road joins from the left.

18.4 Left on State Road 1015 (SR 1015), Oxford Road, at the T.

Oxford Road becomes White Church Road at a stop sign at PA 234, East Berlin Road/Heidlersburg Road, at 19.8 miles.

21.7 Left at the stop sign where Weirman's Road joins from the left.

The road you are on is now called Weirman's Road. Cross a metal grate bridge immediately. Cross the US 15 overpass at 22.2 miles.

22.3 Left on Old Harrisburg Road at the T. York Road is to the right.

22.4 Right on Willow Lane, the next right before crossing the creek. This intersection is unmarked.

24.1 Right on Oxford Road at the T. You will climb a short, steep hill at 25.5 miles.

Apple orchards line both sides of the road at 27 miles.

26.8 Bear left on Idaville York Springs Road at the Y.

28.6 Left on PA 34, York Springs Road, in Idaville.

Cross Bermudian Creek at 28.7 miles.

There are not as many monuments in the East Cavalry Battlefield, but they are no less poignant.

28.9 *Straight to stay on Old Carlisle Road. PA 34 turns right and you will leave the main road.*

35.7 *Straight to join PA 394 at Heidlesburg Road. Cross Conewago Creek at 36.5 miles.*

36.1 *Straight to stay on Table Rock Road. Leave PA 394, Shriver's Corner Road.*

40.7 *Left on PA 34, Biglerville Road, at the T.*

41.4 *Right on West Broadway.*

41.4 *Left on Washington Street.*

This street takes you past Gettysburg College with some lovely Victorian buildings.

41.9 *Left on Chambersburg Road.*

42.0 *End at Lincoln Square.*

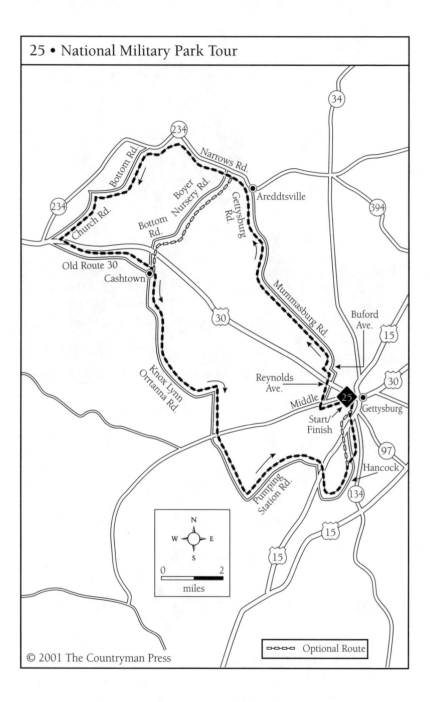

34

234

Bottom Rd.

Narrows Rd.

234

Church Rd.

Boyer Nursery Rd.

Bottom Rd.

Gettysburg Rd.

Areddtsville

394

Old Route 30

Cashtown

30

Mummasburg Rd.

Buford Ave.

15

Knox Lynn Orrtanna Rd.

Reynolds Ave.

Middle

25

30

Gettysburg

Start/Finish

97

Hancock

Pumping Station Rd.

134

N
W ⊕ E
S

0   2
miles

15

15

□□□□ Optional Route

© 2001 The Countryman Press

$$25$$

National Military Park Tour

Distance: *40 miles (optional route 32 miles)*
Difficulty: *Moderate to difficult (optional route moderate)*
Terrain: *Flat to rolling with a 10-mile climb of 600 feet. There is a 0.25-mile section of paved road that is covered by gravel at 13.4 miles. Suitable for any bicycle.*
Optional Route: *I have included an optional route that is flat to rolling, and the long climb and gravel road are eliminated. If you decide to use this route, you will turn on Boyer Nursery Road at 10 miles. You will catch up with the longer route when you arrive at PA 234.*
Location: *Gettysburg is 38 miles southwest of Harrisburg on US 15.*
Services: *You can stop for snacks and drinks in Arendtsville at about 10 miles. There is also a restaurant in Cashtown, about 22 miles along the full route, or 15 miles on the shorter version.*

To Get There

Take I-81 to Harrisburg. Then follow US 15 South. This becomes Carlisle Street, which intersects with US 30, Chambersburg Road, at Lincoln Square.

The Ride

0.0 *Start on the west side of Lincoln Square, heading west on Chambersburg Road, US 30.*

0.1 *Left on Washington Street.*

0.2 *Right on Middle Street.*

You will follow signs for the Gettysburg Battlefield auto tour from here until the turn on Mummasburg Road at 2.9 miles.

1.3 Right on Reynolds Avenue.

This is where the battle of Gettysburg began near McPherson Farm at around 8 AM on July 1, 1863. Cross Chambersburg Road, US 30, at 2 miles.

2.3 Left on Wadsworth Avenue.

2.4 Right on Buford Avenue.

2.9 Left on Mummasburg Road, leaving the auto tour just before the Eternal Light Peace Monument.

In 1938, 1,800 Civil War veterans met here to dedicate this monument to "Peace Eternal in a Nation United."

9.0 Mummasburg Road becomes Gettysburg Road.

9.3 Go straight across Main Street where Gettysburg Road becomes Pearl Street.

This town is Arendtsville. To the left is a gas station with a convenience store.

9.5 Left on Queen Street at the T.

9.6 Right on High Street at the T. This is also PA 254.

9.9 The name changes to Narrows Road.

This lovely road follows Conewago Creek.

10.4 If you wish to follow the shorter, less hilly route, turn left here on Boyer Nursery Road.

See optional route below. Continue straight to complete the full route.

12.3 This is still PA 254, but the name changes to Buchanan Valley Road.

13.4 Left on Bottom Road.

Bottom Road is paved, but covered with gravel for a quarter of a mile.

16.0 Right on New Road.

16.3 Left on Church Road.

18.6 Left on Buchanan Valley Road, PA 254.

MacPherson's Ridge, where the battle of Gettysburg began on July 1, 1863, can be seen on the Auto Tour.

18.7 *Cross Chambersburg Road, US 30. Immediately turn left on Old Route 30.*

22.6 *(Short Route 15.0) Right on Orrtanna Road in Cashtown.*

This is where the short route rejoins the full route. The Cashtown Inn is on the left on Old Route 30 before you turn.

23.7 *(Short Route 16.2) Bear left to stay on Orrtanna Road.*

25.3 *(Short Route 17.7) Left on Knox Lyn Orrtanna Road.*

27.2 *(Short Route 19.6) Left to stay on Knox Lyn Orrtanna Road.*

The Gettysburg KOA campground is to the right on Knox Road about a quarter of a mile.

27.8 *(Short Route 20.2) Right on Knoxlyn Road.*

The names can be confusing here. Straight ahead is Knox Lyn Orrtanna Road. You want Knoxlyn Road.

29.3 *(Short Route 21.7) Straight.*

Cross PA 116, Fairfield Road/Hagerstown Road. Knox Lyn Road becomes Camp Gettysburg Road.

31.6 (Short Route 24.0) Left on Pumping Station Road.

34.4 (Short Route 26.8) Right on Confederate Avenue where you return to the auto tour.

36.3 Warfield Ridge is on the right.

There are picnic tables and toilets. Little Round Top, at 37 miles, was a key stronghold for the Union Army.

37.1 Cross Wheatfield Road.

Here Confederate Avenue becomes Sedgewick Avenue.

37.6 The name changes to Hancock Avenue.

38.7 (Short Route 31.1) Right into the parking lot of the Cyclorama.

This is the end of the auto tour. Ride through the Cyclorama parking lot.

38.8 (Short Route 31.2) Left on PA 134, Taneytown Road.

39.1 (Short Route 31.5) Cross US 15, Steinwehr Avenue, where Taneytown Road becomes Washington Street.

39.8 (Short Route 32.2) Right on Chambersburg Road, US 30.

39.9 (Short Route 32.3) End at Lincoln Square.

Optional Route

10.3 Right at Boyer's Nursery Road.

12.9 Right where Boyer's Nursery Road ends and becomes Cashtown Road, joining from the left.

13.9 Left at the T on High Street. Cross US 30, Chambersburg Road, at 14.2 miles.

14.9 Left on Old Route 30 in Cashtown.

The Cashtown Inn is one block to your right.

15.0 Right on Orrtanna Road and continue the full route. Miles are shown as follows: (Short Route 21.6).

Let Backcountry Guides Take You There

Our experienced backcountry authors will lead you to the finest trails, parks, and back roads in the following areas:

25 Bicycle Tours Series

25 Bicycle Tours in the Adirondacks
25 Bicycle Tours on Delmarva
25 Bicycle Tours in Savannah and the
  Carolina Low Country
25 Bicycle Tours in Maine
25 Bicycle Tours in Maryland
25 Bicycle Tours in the Twin Cities and
  Southeastern Minnesota
30 Bicycle Tours in New Jersey
30 Bicycle Tours in the Finger Lakes Region
25 Bicycle Tours in the Hudson Valley
25 Bicycle Tours in Ohio's Western Reserve
25 Bicycle Tours in the Texas Hill Country and
  West Texas
25 Bicycle Tours in Vermont
25 Bicycle Tours in and around Washington, D.C.
30 Bicycle Tours in Wisconsin
25 Mountain Bike Tours in the Adirondacks
25 Mountain Bike Tours in the Hudson Valley
25 Mountain Bike Tours in Massachusetts
25 Mountain Bike Tours in New Jersey
25 Mountain Bike Tours in Vermont
Backroad Bicycling in Connecticut
Backroad Bicycling on Cape Cod, Martha's Vineyard, and Nantucket
The Mountain Biker's Guide to Ski Resorts

Bicycling America's National Parks Series

Bicycling America's National Parks:
  Arizona & New Mexico
Bicycling America's National Parks: California
Bicycling America's National Parks:
  Oregon & Washington
Bicycling America's National Parks:
  Utah & Colorado

50 Hikes Series

50 Hikes in the Adirondacks
50 Hikes in Connecticut
50 Hikes in the Maine Mountains
50 Hikes in Coastal and Southern Maine
50 Hikes in Maryland
50 Hikes in Massachusetts
50 Hikes in Michigan
50 Hikes in the White Mountains
50 More Hikes in New Hampshire
50 Hikes in New Jersey
50 Hikes in Central New York
50 Hikes in Western New York
50 Hikes in the Mountains of North Carolina
50 Hikes in Ohio
50 Hikes in Eastern Pennsylvania
50 Hikes in Central Pennsylvania
50 Hikes in Western Pennsylvania
50 Hikes in the Tennessee Mountains
50 Hikes in Vermont
50 Hikes in Northern Virginia

Walks and Rambles Series

Walks and Rambles on Cape Cod and the Islands
Walks and Rambles on the Delmarva Peninsula
Walks and Rambles in the Western
  Hudson Valley
Walks and Rambles on Long Island
Walks and Rambles in Ohio's Western Reserve
Walks and Rambles in Rhode Island
Walks and Rambles in and around St. Louis

We offer many more books on hiking, fly-fishing, travel, nature, and other subjects. Our books are available at bookstores and outdoor stores everywhere. For more information or a free catalog, please call 1-800-245-4151 or write to us at The Countryman Press, P.O. Box 748, Woodstock, Vermont 05091. You can find us on the Internet at http://www.countrymanpress.com.